THE HUMAN RIGHTS
OF
PROFESSIONAL
HELPERS

THE HUMAN RIGHTS
OF
PROFESSIONAL
HELPERS

By

GEORGE HENDERSON, Ph.D.

S.N. Goldman Professor of Human Relations
Professor of Education and Associate Professor
of Sociology
University of Oklahoma
Norman, Oklahoma

CHARLES C THOMAS • PUBLISHER
Springfield • Illinois • U.S.A.

Published and Distributed Throughout the World by

CHARLES C THOMAS • PUBLISHER
2600 South First Street
Springfield, Illinois, 62717, U.S.A.

© *1983 by* CHARLES C THOMAS • PUBLISHER

ISBN 0-398-04820-7

Library of Congress Catalog Card Number: 82-19684

With THOMAS BOOKS *careful attention is given to all details of
manufacturing and design. It is the Publisher's desire to present books that
are satisfactory as to their physical qualities and artistic possibilities and
appropriate for their particular use.* THOMAS BOOKS *will be true to those
laws of quality that assure a good name and good will.*

Printed in the United States of America

I-R-1

Library of Congress Cataloging in Publication Data

Henderson, George, 1932 —
    The human rights of professional helpers.

    Bibliography: p.
    Includes index.
    1. Social workers — Civil rights — United States.
2.   Social workers — United States — Attitudes.
3.   Interpersonal relations. I. Title.
HV10.5.H4 1983   361.3'01'9   82-19684
ISBN 0-398-04820-7

To George, Jr., Michele, Faith, Lea, Joy, Lisa, and Dawn—who helped me to grow up.

PREFACE

A BILL of human rights needs to be drafted for professional helpers. All too frequently human service workers assume that someone else will take care of their ailing or disgruntled colleagues. Equally presumptuous, they judge coworkers harshly when they do not meet their expectations. And, yes, they ridicule, lecture, and force coworkers to conform to agency norms. Often they delay solutions, forgetting that a colleague's pain does not end while they are procrastinating and avoiding the human encounter. The words of Jean de Rougemont are prophetic: "Man seeks man and flees from him."*

Moral and social interventions are aspects of our personal and professional growth. Indeed, they are integral components of our interpersonal relationships. However, it is important to keep in mind that these interventions should not come in the form of coercion or neglect. Caring, like commitment, requires a sharing of the human experience, but first we must care for ourselves, not in order to exclude others but in order to nourish ourselves. When we venture outside our skin, generally it is easier to care for strangers than our colleagues, who are likely to see through our plastic professional veneers.

Some workers are treated as if their feelings do not exist, and their behavior is seen as originating not in their own free consciousness but elsewhere — in someone else's mind. Thus, their pain is dismissed as hypochondria, their allegations of discrimination are believed to be unfounded, and their personal worth is grossly underestimated.

---

*Jean de Rougemont. Quoted in Paul Tournier: *The Meaning of Persons* (New York: Harper & Row, 1957, p.32).

Many helping personnel behave as if they are hopelessly insensitive to the plight of their colleagues. The irony of this situation is immediately apparent. Taught to be empathic and caring—even non-discriminatory in ethnic and gender interactions — these paragons of professional virtue model what one should *not* do in the helping relationship. Some helpers stand shocked, wide-eyed, and immobilized by their colleagues' pain and imperfections. Indeed, many helpers assume a posture of untrained, traumatized innocents when a coworker cries out for help.

As if under a spell, some human service agency personnel run aimlessly from one ailing colleague to another without adequately helping anyone. Some helpers even believe their afflicted colleagues —especially women, ethnic minorities, alcoholics, older persons, mentally and terminally ill—are beyond help.

When lay persons behave in this manner, it is reprehensible. When professionals behave this way, it is inexcusable and reprehensible. There is no professional code of helping that extends assistance to strangers but not one's colleagues. Perhaps it is the frantic pace of day-to-day agency activities that causes such behavior. Perhaps it is oversight. Whatever the case, not even the most plausible and probable reasons can mollify human service workers whose cries for help have gone unanswered.

The conditions I have described exist in all helping professions, including social work, human relations, education, clinical psychology, public administration, and criminal justice. In an effort to seek solutions, I have drawn many of the ideas found in this book from several academic disciplines. However, this is not a book focusing on placing blame. Instead, I have tried to identify problems, define them, and present possible solutions. Specifically, this is a book designed for instruction in all human service-oriented curricula and in-service training programs. No doubt the greatest use for *The Human Rights of Professional Helpers* will be as an addition to the personal and professional libraries of human service personnel.

For those of us who care, the options are clear: we can either hire out as mourners as our colleagues lose their positions or we can become actively involved in preventing and helping to abate their problems. We must become the kind of activists Malcolm Boyd described:

Shallow activism must ... be changed into a considerably deeper and more sophisticated sense of involvement. This calls for listening to people outside one's own ingrown and myopic clique as well as sober examination of self righteousness in one's motives and actions .... A realist throws away rose-colored glasses, straightens his shoulders and looks freely about him in all directions. He wants to see whatever there is to see, in relation to other people and things as well as to himself. A realist alone comprehends hope. Optimism is as antithetical to authentic hope as pessimism. Hope is rooted in realism.*

Although they usually try, helpers do not remain detached, objective, and neutral—far from it, for they are, first of all, human beings with their own values, attitudes, and beliefs. I have tried to place my concepts of helping the helpers within this complex framework. There is always the danger that we will become what we do not want to be: insensitive to the plight of our colleagues. Therefore, a major theme throughout this book is that we must always choose deliberate deception over self-deception. By being honest with ourselves we have the best chance of retaining mastery over our own tactics.

I have, in summary, attempted to open up a dialogue and prompt a series of helping behaviors. If only one person is helped by someone who reads this book, my energy was well spent. In my wildest fantasy, *The Human Rights of Professional Helpers* becomes a foundation upon which other books are written.

I am indebted to many persons for the material that follows. The foremost contributors were members of my graduate seminars focusing on human resources development: Karen Crane, Ruth Domin, Anthony Garcia, Frederick Hushbeck, William Lynd, Susan Slopey, Gary Stinnett, Winifred Strider, Sharon Wade, and Pamela Westbrook. Their critiques and reports helped me to move from ideas to written pages.

G.H.

---

*Malcolm Boyd: *Human Like Me, Jesus* (New York: Simon & Schuster, 1971, p. 128).

CONTENTS

THE HUMAN RIGHTS
OF
PROFESSIONAL
HELPERS

Chapter 1
SALVAGING WASTED PEOPLE

AN organization is only as effective as the people who operate it. Too many human service agencies are similar to a malnourished body. They look healthy to untrained eyes, but in reality they are sick and decaying inside. The laughter and incessant chatter frequently hide a series of disruptive problems. Like vaudevillian actors, agency personnel in need of help typically push aside their own pain as they take their agency-helping shows on the road. In most instances, there is little or no help for ailing helpers. This is not because the other agency personnel do not want to help. Many of them do, but few of them know how to help their colleagues.

I have described a nontherapeutic situation in therapeutic agencies. The question becomes, Who will help the ailing helpers? The answer, while less obvious, is, With more training, help can come from administrators, colleagues, and the workers themselves. Among the activities that will allow a positive resolution of intrapersonal, interpersonal, and intergroup problems are: listening, reflecting, and interpreting; rewarding positive behavior; directly or symbolically satisfying the most crucial workers' needs; respecting rather than "using" people; encouraging and permitting free emotional expression; continually monitoring the agency's human relations climate.

Administrator Hang-ups

The collective attempt of the human race to understand its existence is a classical study in frustration. *Homo sapiens* has always been concerned with structuring universal reality not only tempo-

3

rarily but ultimately. Our confrontations with the universe arouse complex emotions within us. That is, most people are puzzled by cyclic patterns of the seasons, the unerring polarities of days and nights, the conflict between reason and emotion, the glorious process of birth, and the inevitable call of death. In short, human life seems to have complexity beyond our power of total comprehension, and yet human service agencies are trying to understand and control it.

Perhaps the most difficult topics for agency administrators are those dealing with subordinate complaints, inadequacies, failures, and dismissals. Some administrators believe that they must save every person—even those labeled "terminal." Unaware of how much perfection they demand of themselves, these administrators consider all the problems of their staff as their own. Indeed, staff failures are painful reminders of their own vulnerability. Ergo, when possible, thoughts of staff shortcomings are pushed into the unconscious realms of their minds. As a whole, human service agency administrators—like physicians—provide little room in their activities for failure or the natural and inevitable processes of dying and death. Staff members whose major discomforts center on equity, therapy, and cure have great difficulty discussing these things with most administrators, who when confronted become defensive and tend to do a considerable amount of public and private grieving.

The grieving administrator typically tries to delay, to deny, and refute the possibility of losing valued staff members. No matter how many times one has the experience, it is not easy to take for granted the loss of productive individuals. While not a rigid order of events, grieving administrators (similar to individuals grieving the loss of loved ones in a family) tend to follow this sequence: (1) shock and disbelief, (2) conscious awareness of the impending loss, (3) mourning, and (4) resolution. Some individuals never reach the last stage. Until administrators receive adequate course work and clinical experiences focusing on staff grievances and maladjustments, a large number of valuable human resources will be needlessly wasted.

It is important that administrators do not prematurely give up their ailing staff members to failure or death. Knowing what is wrong with an individual is a mixed bag of knowledge. There is a great temptation to calculate the odds against successful conciliation or rehabilitation. It seems almost patronizing to admonish administrators to use statistics with great care; yet, the warning is necessary. For instance, it is impossible to make a knowledgeable prediction about a staff member's chances of recovering from an illness without knowing how he or she compares with the norm and also what his or her physical resources are. In blunt terms, it is better to focus on steps that can be taken to help staff members rather than to make them part of a human lottery.

Only by coming to terms with the feelings that confrontive or ailing staff members arouse in them will administrators be optimally responsive to individual staff needs. Inability to do so may result, for example, in an administrator incorrectly telling an alcoholic that he can handle a drink or two at an agency party or telling a terminally ill person that she "will recover" or "be all right." On the other hand, it is important to note that maladjusted staff members or individuals discriminated against should not be treated like all other staff members. They need special attention.

Administrators should be sensitive to the needs of staff members in pain. All persons in pain—physical or mental—have the right to grieve. Somehow the administrator must be able to communicate to staff members that it is all right to grieve, but away from clients. A more controversial issue is the administrator's right to grieve. It is erroneous to assume that administrators must be superhuman persons insensitive to the suffering around them. However, the appropriate place for administrators to grieve seems to be away from both staff and clients.

HATEFUL STAFF MEMBERS. Because of the way they look, smell, talk, or behave, some staff members frustrate or irritate administrators. Individuals who do not fit the constantly shifting and highly subjective normative characteristics of "good" staff are labeled "problems," "undesirable," and "hateful." When these persons get in trouble or become sick, administrators are not very empathic or forgiving. On the contrary, they don't grieve, they rejoice!

Undesirable staff members fit five categories: socially undesirable, attitudinally undesirable, physically undesirable, circumstantially undesirable, and incidentally undesirable.[1] *Socially undesir-able* staff members include individuals who are alcoholics, members of ethnic minority (or majority) groups, and those who are crude in behavior. *Attitudinally undesirable* staff members are individuals who are ungrateful or arrogant: those who think they "know it all." *Physically undesirable* staff members include individuals who have identifiable physical illnesses, especially chronic illnesses. Sometimes staff members are *circumstantially undesirable* because of situations totally apart from them and beyond their control. Examples of circumstantially undesirable persons include individuals who replace a popular staff member and those who are assigned irritating tasks (e.g. budget monitors).

Some staff members who admit that they have physical or mental problems behave like the patients whom James Groves labeled "hateful." They especially irritate administrators, and such persons fall into four classes: (1) dependent clingers, (2) entitled demanders, (3) manipulative help-rejectors, and (4) self-destructive deniers.

> Clingers escalate from mild and appropriate requests for reassurance to repeated perfervid, incarcerating cries for explanation, affection, analgesics, sedatives and all forms of attention imaginative . . . . Demanders resemble clingers in the profundity of their neediness, but they differ in that—rather than flattery and unconscious seduction—they use intimidation, devaluation and guilt-induction to place the doctor in the role of the inexhaustible supply depot . . . . Help-rejectors, or "crocks," are familiar to every practicing physician. Like clingers and demanders, they appear to have a quenchless need for emotional supplies. Unlike clingers, they are not seductive and grateful; unlike demanders, they are not overtly hostile. They actually seem the opposite of entitled; they appear to feel that no regimen will help . . . . Self-destructive deniers display unconsciously self-murderous behaviors, such as continued drinking of a patient with esophageal varices and hepatic failure.[2]

Male administrators must guard against stereotyping female employees as being hateful persons with mainly psychogenic rather than physiologic illnesses, while male employees are thought to have "real" illnesses. Even if this were true (and it is not), pain is no less real if it has a psychological rather than physical origin. Therefore, it is best not to label employees' illnesses as real or imagined. One approach to the helping relationship is for administrators to apply *reality therapy* as proposed by William Glasser.[3] According to Glasser, administrators must be concerned with providing their employees' needs: the need to love and to be loved and the need to feel that they are worthwhile to themselves and others. If these needs are not fulfilled, worker alienation will result. The love that I am talking about is the biblical love of our neighbors.

Instead of searching for places or persons to lay blame, it is more productive to help employees examine their daily activities and suggest better ways for them to behave, solve problems, or approach people. In the words of Glasser, "Once involvement is gained and reality is faced, therapy becomes a special kind of education, a learning to live more effectively."[4] This is nothing more than good therapy. It is administrators helping their colleagues "meet a problem, fill a need, receive a service. The means to their purpose are the mobilization of dormant capacities in the individual, or the mobilization or appropriate community resources, or both, depending on the needs of each worker."[5]

The core material of this helping relationship is interaction of the basic attitudes and emotions of administrators and their colleagues. Both parties need (1) to be treated as individuals, (2) to be allowed to express feelings, (3) to receive empathic responses to problems, (4) to be judged fairly, and (5) to have their secrets kept.

Barriers to Communication

Human service workers continually debate whether their supervisors and colleagues should be told the "truth" about their health conditions. In addition to being threatening, the truth of a situation is relative. Like all science, medicine is based on probability. A physician may be able to predict that the chances are 99 out of 100 that a given patient will experience certain specific physiological outcomes. But even here the imprecision of science is evident. A physician cannot say with certainty which patient will be the one case that is the exception to the prediction. Furthermore, because human conditions are not static, change is possible. Thus, today's truth may become tomorrow's lie. Ailing persons tend to cling to the hope of a miraculous cure. Thus, many workers hide their illness and pray for a miracle.

Communicating information about one's illness has other problems. We can never be sure how people will interpret our situation. Even professionals familiar with the illness attach different meanings to words. This is especially true of words associated with dreaded or socially taboo sicknesses. For example, cancer and alcoholism have negative connotations to most lay persons – and many professionals, too. Using the best words is an art that few persons of any profession have mastered. Yet it is clear that one's supervisors and colleagues have the right to know something about one's illness. The question is, *What* do they have the right to know?

Going back to my example, to many persons "cancer" means terminal illness and a long, painful death, with no hope of escaping either the disease or the treatment. Specific, concrete descriptions of the cancer (e.g. stage of development and treatment) are less likely to be misunderstood or to leave one's supervisors and colleagues to their fantasies. A general rule of thumb seems to be that mentally and physically ailing professionals give simple explanations to colleagues who ask about their symptoms or treatment, and they give little or no information to others. Individuals who have worked together for a long time in an agency become like a family and, as extended relatives, they prefer (1) to know a colleague's prognosis, (2) to have their questions answered honestly, (3) to know specific facts concerning their colleague's progress, (4) to receive periodic progress reports, and (5) to have explanations of the illness given in terms that are understandable.[6]

> The historical record indicates physicians have recognized that words can wound as deeply as knives, that what is said can be as significant as what is done. Those who argue that disclosure of threatening news should be the rule rather than the exception bear weighty burdens. They must have prepared themselves to learn spoken and silent cues patients telegraph about facts they know or crave about their illnesses, to communicate effectively with patients and sustain them emotionally once the news is out, to understand psychological difficulties that can accompany disclosure, and to allocate time for the often lengthy period over which disclosure can take place. They must also recognize that the harm created by inadequate mastery of the techniques and skills of communicating bad news may outweigh the benefits to the individual of learning the truth.[7]

Usually the ailing worker must send the first message of communication, which simply stated is "Help me, I am sick." Most professionals are hesitant to admit that *they* need help. Yet, only after being told by their colleagues that they are sick can they comfortably adopt the ailing role. It is no secret that administrators have power over their subordinates. Supervisors who are authoritarian and dominating are the most difficult persons to tell about our illness. Those who are democratic encourage such disclosures.

Most human service agency messages follow the classic power flow interaction process:

1. Communication flows more readily laterally between administrators or between subordinates than either downward from supervisors to subordinates or upward from subordinates to supervisors.
2. More communication of illnesses goes from subordinates to supervisors than from supervisors to subordinates.
3. Subordinates are more cautious than supervisors about the messages they send.
4. Supervisors and subordinates incorrectly assume the extent that their illnesses are understood by each other.
5. All employees tend to avoid talking about their illnesses.

Part of the administrator's dilemma is that he or she must be sufficiently detached from subordinates to exercise sound judgment and at the same time have enough concern for them to provide sensitive, empathic support. It is possible for an administrator to suppress on the conscious level emotional responses while counseling angry or ailing colleagues, but this detachment does not remove the stress and concern hidden in the unconscious domain of the mind. The pathological process of detachment which produces mature administrators also has the tendency to produce cynical clinicians.

Helping colleagues to report civil rights violations or to tell what ails them requires more than a receptive listener. Those who believe that the structured interview is the only effective method have lost touch with basic social work methodology.

It has long been said in casework, reiterated against the sometime
practice of subjecting the client to a barrage of ready-made questions, that the client should be allowed to tell his story in his own
way. Particularly at the beginning this is true, because the client may
feel an urgency to do just that, to pour out what *he* sees and thinks
and feels because it is his problem and because he has lived with it
and mulled it within himself for days or perhaps months. Moreover,
it is his own way that gives both caseworker and client not just the
objective facts of the problem but the grasp of its significance. To
the client who is ready and able to give out with what troubles him,
the caseworker's nods and murmurs of understanding – any of those
nonverbal ways by which we indicate response – may be all the client
needs in his first experience of telling and being heard out.[8]

Few people know exactly how they feel about what is bother-
ing them until they have communicated sufficient data to someone else—a spouse or a colleague. To tell their colleagues what we
are feeling about job-related problems is in itself a relief for most
workers, but telling is not enough. An adjustment, a cure, or rehabilitation must follow. Typical questions raised by human service professionals include the following:

- What is wrong with me (you)?
- What's going to happen to me (you)?
- What can I (you) do to help?

The words of Paul Tournier sum up the process of helping a
troubled colleague to communicate: "Through information I can
understand a case, only through communication shall I be able to
understand a person. . . . "[9] Comments such as "I imagine that this
is not easy for you to talk about" or "Go on, I'm listening" may
be enough encouragement for reticent colleagues. Others will need
direct questions to help them focus their conversation. One of the
most difficult and important professional helper roles is that of
listener. It is even more difficult when a friend is ailing.

The first rule of helper communication is that the helper should
understand the helpee's values. The second rule is that the helper
should adapt his or her communicative behavior to the helpee's
value systems. This implies respect for different gender and cultural values, but it does not mean "talking down" to or patronizing
colleagues. Agency directors and supervisors should:

- Receive the aggrieved or ailing person's messages with open minds.
- Listen, read, or observe the entire communication—verbal/nonverbal.
- Seek clarification of ambiguous messages.
- Validate asserted facts and seek missing information.

The communication task is formidable: aggrieved or ailing persons must be given the best chance of resolving the problem and the least chance of disillusionment. This, of course, is the perennial problem of humanely managing the living, consoling the dying, and giving dignity to those who are to be terminated. Clearly, considerable human relations skills are needed to perform these tasks.

Leadership Constraints

A number of constraints act on agency supervisors during the course of their jobs and inhibit them from being optimally supportive of their subordinates. One of the constraints is inherent in human service institutions and community expectations of financial prudence. This leads many administrators to fire, lay off, or force the early retirement of employees needing equity adjustments or extensive medical care. When forced to choose between saving people or saving money, most administrators opt for the latter. Furthermore, evidence indicates that generally there is a goal conflict between supervisors and subordinates. Most administrators are *task* oriented—that is, they want the jobs to get done. Most subordinates are *process* oriented—they want empathy, warmth, and consideration from their supervisors. Thus, a supervisor is likely to ask a worker who has filed a discrimination complaint, "Will you be able to finish the assignment?"; while the worker is likely to ask, "Do you think I should be doing this assignment?"

Basically, two terms are paramount in analyzing a human service agency's leadership style: (1) consideration and (2) initiating structure. *Consideration* means administrators will take care of their subordinates, who want supervisors to reward them for good job performance, to stand up for them, to be approachable, and to assist them in the solution of personal problems. Above all else, agency personnel want their supervisors to accept their grievances and their illnesses without being punitive.

Initiating structure is another way of saying "getting the job done with people in mind." Specifically, it involves defining a mission, organizing the tasks to be accomplished, and devising methods to perform them. It includes such specifics as establishing organization patterns, developing two-way channels of communication, and assigning specific tasks to individuals. One common error in selecting agency goals is the belief that concern for mission achievement and concern for people are mutually contradictory. There is no effective yardstick of leadership with consideration of individuals at the one end and accomplishment of missions at the other. The good administrator will satisfy both.

If administrators are to be mediators between themselves and their subordinates, this function must be recognized at all levels of the agency structure and it must be translated into general policy guidelines. Unrealistic policies and regulations only serve to alienate agency personnel. The human relations climate of an agency can be measured by the following:

1. *Structure*: the feeling workers have about the freedom or constraints of their work situation.
2. *Responsibility*: the feeling of being in control and not having to "run upstairs" everytime a decision must be made.
3. *Risk*: the degree to which staff members feel they can initiate job improvement.
4. *Standards*: the extent to which challenging goals are set for each worker; that is, the emphasis staff members feel is being placed on doing the best possible job.
5. *Reward*: the degree to which agency personnel feel they are rewarded for good work rather than only being blamed when something goes wrong.
6. *Support*: the perceived amount of helpfulness of supervisors and colleagues in accomplishing tasks.
7. *Conflict*: the feeling of staff members that administrators do or do not want to hear different opinions to get internal problems out in the open where they can be dealt with.

8. *Warmth*: the feeling of "fellowship" or lack of it that prevails in the agency.
9. *Identity*: the degree to which individual workers feel that they are members of the agency "family" and belong.

It should be clear by now that regardless of how much power or formal authority an organization confers on its administrators, *usable* power and authority are granted by their subordinates. A human relations approach to leadership is gaining acceptance in human service agencies and is being implemented in some places to winnow common goals from contradictory points of view. Rap sessions, films and speakers with well-defined messages, and carefully controlled role playing are but a few of many in-service activities available to administrators endeavoring to create viable organizations with minimum stress.

There is a new spirit among agency administrators who dare to innovate and deviate from tradition in order to solve problems that have no guiding precedent. The rigid conformist and the technocratic midget are on the way out, as is the empathy distance between supervisors and subordinates. Human service agency leadership is not a spectator sport; the best and the worst of persons enter the arena. Albert Schweitzer's message is appropriate: "Let those who hold the fates of people in their hands be careful to avoid everything which may worsen our situation or make it more perilous. Let them take to heart the marvelous words of the Apostle Paul: As much as lies in you, be at peace with all men. They have meaning, not only for individuals, but also for nations."[10]

Sometimes agencies resemble nations whose citizens are at war with each other. The wounded become alcoholics, develop ulcers, acquire mental problems, or burn out. Those fatally injured lose their jobs or die on the job. Agencies of this kind desperately need to be at peace with themselves. No agency should be a battlefield, but many of them are. Needless to say, these institutions need the best possible administrators.

Prelude to Helping

Most workers' problems are rooted in their social environments. Certainly family or group therapy is an alternative. Another alternative is social action designed to change their jobs. One of the reasons teachers, social workers, and other human service personnel are continually frustrated is because the problems they are called upon to solve are themselves the products of a larger social environment that includes their agencies.

Frequently, an ailing worker's rehabilitation or recovery depends not on his or her adjustment to an existing agency situation but instead on being moved to another job or another agency. This kind of environmental change is not without a theoretical foundation: it is modeled after milieu therapy and community or social psychiatry. Patterns of human relationships are consciously attuned to the treatment needs of the agency workers. It is clear that many agency personnel do not get the institutional help they need because agency resources are not attuned to their needs. The more effective helpers behave in the following manner:

1. They regard each colleague as a vital part of the agency.
2. They view all personnel positively, because whatever diminishes anyone's self (e.g. humiliation, discrimination, degradation, failure) has no place in a helping agency.
3. They allow and provide for individual differences.
4. They learn how things are seen by their colleagues.

Since sensitivity to their own feelings is a prerequisite to effective helping, it is beneficial for administrators to have maximum self-insight. For some administrators, this is an integral part of their personality; for others, it must be learned. A growing number of agency administrators are participating in some type of sensitivity training.

If it is true that helping can be accomplished only with the assistance of a healthier person, then it is imperative that administrators "have themselves together." An alcoholic does not need guidance from an administrator who also is unable to stop drinking. Nor does a burned-out employee need a burned-out supervisor. The type of administrator I am encouraging is a mature person who functions with compassionate efficiency, and he or she is able to assist colleagues to solve their problems without resorting to pity, panic, or resignation. This type of administrator maintains professional balance and keeps his or her perspective through the use of insight and humor.

The helping relationship has qualities that are the same whether it is between social worker and client, counselor and counselee, or teacher and student. The psychological equilibrium underlying the occupational roles resides at a much deeper, more fundamental level than a list of behaviors learned in a college class. Effective help at the emotional level is initiated not so much by technique or special knowledge of the different professions but rather by the positive attitude of the helper. It is important to note that experienced helpers without college degrees may have a better conception of what constitutes a helping relationship than their colleagues who have mastered the theoretical concepts but have little practical experience.

Some human service professionals see the helping process as one in which they make intricate diagnoses of their ailing colleagues and define them as being "sick" and themselves as being "well." In actuality, most of us have been or will be ill. When William Menninger was asked how many people suffer from emotional illness, he answered, "One out of one of us." With this thought in mind, all of us must be aware of the times when we cannot help others because we are in need of help ourselves. Carl Rogers listed four attitudinal characteristics of effective helpers who counsel their colleagues: (1) they manifest empathic understanding; (2) they have unconditional positive regard for their colleagues; (3) they are genuine or congruent (that is, their behavior matches their feelings); and (4) their responses match their colleagues' statements in intensity and affective expression.[11]

Effective helpers can convey genuineness, empathy, and unconditional positive regard through four statements, including the feelings and actions that accompany them: "This is it," "I know that it must hurt," "I am here to help you if you want me and can use me," and "You don't have to face this alone." According to Alan Keith-Lucas, "Reality without empathy is harsh and unhelpful. Empathy about something that is not real is clearly meaningless and can only lead the client to what we have called nonchoice. Reality and empathy together need support, both material and psychological, if decisions are to be carried out. Support in carrying out unreal plans is obviously a waste of time."[12]

Lest human service personnel think that they must single-handedly bear the burden of helping ailing colleagues, I remind them of three widely held assumptions about the universality of helping: (1) we all at times have emotional problems that we experience as unpleasant and painful; (2) we all seek help for our personal and professional problems; and (3) we all offer help to others who are experiencing emotional difficulties. The help we all seek may come from a spouse, a parent, a colleague, or a stranger. Whenever possible, agency problems should be solved by agency personnel.

Once a problem is identified, administrators should move with great care when implementing change. Some actions, although well intentioned, will only exacerbate the problem. Anything that disrupts the existing flow of work activities can cause additional complaints, stresses, and illnesses. This is especially true when the following conditions occur:

1. *When the purpose of the change is not made clear.* Suspense and anxiety are caused by mystery and ambiguity. Fear of change can be as disrupting as change itself. Administrators trying to help colleagues discriminated against or ailing should make their reasons and intentions clear. Otherwise, all workers may see a Machiavellian plot where none is intended.

2. *When persons affected by the change are not involved in the planning.* People tend to support what they help plan and to resist what is imposed by others. Involving agency personnel in plans to assist a colleague will be better received than a memorandum soliciting cooperation.

3. *When the habit patterns of work groups are ignored.* Every work situation develops unique ways of doing things. The administrator who ignores institutionalized patterns of work and abruptly attempts to restructure them is likely to run into resistance. This is true even when reordering the pattern of an ill person to prolong his or her job usefulness.

4. *When there is poor communication regarding the change.* Agency personnel expect, need, and want to be informed about changes *before* they occur.

5. *When excessive work pressure is involved.* Frequently, such pressure results when administrators do not plan changes far enough in advance or are uneasy about these changes themselves.
6. *When anxiety over job security is not relieved.* Aggrieved and ailing staff members, as well as those who are not, need to know what is going to happen to them. Individuals or subunits of an organization will try to protect themselves and their "empires."

It should be clear that the task of salvaging wasted human resources is neither easy nor always understood and appreciated, but it should be done. Not only is this good human relations, it is good business. The chapters that follow will focus on specific human resources development issues.

EXERCISE DRILL

"Please Hear What I'm Not Saying"

Don't be fooled by me.
Don't be fooled by the face I wear.
For I wear a mask, a thousand masks,
    masks that I'm afraid to take off
    and none of them are me.
Pretending is an art that's second nature with me,
    But don't be fooled, for God's sake, don't be fooled.
I give you the impression that I'm secure,
    that all is sunny and unruffled with me,
    within as well as without,
    that confidence is my name and coolness is my game,
    that the water's calm, and I'm in command,
    that I need no one.
But don't believe me.
Please.
My surface may seem smooth, but my surface is my mask,
    of my ever-varying and ever-concealing mask.
Beneath lies no smugness, no complacence,
Beneath lies the real me in confusion, in defeat, in aloneness.
But I hide this.
I don't want anybody to know it.

I panic at the thought of my weakness and fear being exposed.
That's why I frantically create a mask to hide behind,
    a nonchalant, sophisticated facade, to help me pretend,
    to shield me from the glance that knows.
But such a glance is precisely my salvation. My only salvation.
And I know it.
That is if it's followed by acceptance, if it's followed by love.
It's the only thing that can liberate me, from myself,
    from my own self-built prison walls,
    from the barriers that I do painstakingly erect.
It's the only thing that will assure me of what I can't assure
    myself,
    that I'm really worth something.
But I don't tell you this, I don't dare to. I'm afraid to.
I'm afraid you'll think less of me, that you'll laugh,
    and your laugh would kill me.
So I play my game, my desperate pretending game,
    with a facade of assurance without, and a trembling
    child within.
And so begins the parade of masks,
    the glittering-by, empty parade of masks . . . .
And my life become a front.
I idly chatter to you in the suave tone of surface talk.
I tell you everything that's really nothing,
    and nothing of what's everything, of what's crying
    within me.
So when I'm going through my routine do not be fooled by
    what I'm saying.
Please listen carefully and try to hear what I'm NOT saying,
    what I'd like to be able to say, what for survival I
    need to say,
    but what I can't say.
I dislike hiding. Honestly.
I dislike the superficial game I'm playing, the superficial,
    phony game.
I'd really like to be genuine and spontaneous, and me.
But you've got to help me.
You've got to hold out your hand
    even when that's the last thing I seem to want, or need.
Only you can call me to aliveness.
Only you can wipe away from my eyes the blank stare

of the breathing dead.
Each time you're kind, and gentle, and encouraging,
    each time you try to understand because you really care,
    my heart begins to grow wings, very small wings, very
    feeble wings,
    but wings.
With your sensitivity and sympathy, and your power of understanding,
    you can breathe life into me. I want you to know that.
I want you to know how important you are to me, how you can be
    a creator of the person that is me if you choose to.
Please choose to.
You alone can break down the wall behind which I tremble.
You alone can release me from my shadow world of panic and
    uncertainty,
    from my lonely prison.
So do not pass me by.
It will not be easy for you.
A long conviction of worthlessness builds strong walls.
The nearer you approach me, the blinder I may strike back.
It's irrational, but despite what the books say about man,
    I am irrational.
I fight against the very thing that I cry out for. But I am
    told that love is stronger than strong walls, and in
    this lies my hope,
    my only hope.
Please try to beat down those walls with firm hands, but
    with gentle hands for a child is very sensitive.
Who am I, you may wonder? I am someone you know very well.
For I am every man you meet and I am every woman you meet.

Anonymous

1. What part(s) of "Please Hear What I'm Not Saying" have special meaning for you? Why?
2. Think of someone whom you dislike. Does this poem give you another perspective of that person? If so, describe it.

REFERENCES

1. Papper, S.: The undesirable patient. *Journal of Chronic Diseases, 22*: 771–779, 1970.
2. Groves, J.E.: Taking care of the hateful patient. *New England Journal of Medicine, 291*:305, 1974.

3. Glasser, W.: *Reality Therapy.* New York: Harper & Row, 1965.

4. Ibid., p. 60.

5. Biestek, F.P.: *The Casework Relationship.* Chicago: Loyola University Press, 1956, p. 3.

6. Molter, N.C.: Needs of relatives of critically ill patients: A descriptive study. *Heart and Lung, 8*:334, 1979.

7. Reiser, S.J.: Words as scalpels: Transmitting evidence in the clinical dialogue. *Annals of Internal Medicine, 92*:840–841, 1980.

8. Perlman, H.H.: *Social Casework: A Problem-Solving Process.* Chicago: University of Chicago Press, 1957, p. 142.

9. Tournier, P.: *The Meaning of Persons.* New York: Harper & Row, 1957, p. 25.

10. Schweitzer, A.: *Pilgrimage to Humanity.* Translated by Walter E. Stuermann. New York: Philosophical Library, 1961, p. 100.

11. Rogers, C.R.: The process equation of psychotherapy. *American Journal of Psychotherapy, 15*:27–45, 1961.

12. Keith-Lucas, A.: *Giving and Taking Help.* Chapel Hill: University of North Carolina Press, 1972, p. 88.

Chapter 2
BURNED OUT

THE human being is an amazingly adaptive organism. However, under conditions of physical and psychological stress, survival adjustments can be impeded and ultimately, if it is extreme, we will die. *Stress refers to any assault or demand placed on a person or system.* Perhaps what I have described are conditions of modern urban living, or as Louis Kaplan observed: "Despite the fact that they spend a large proportion of their time among other people, this relationship is often impersonal and mechanical. Many people are merely cogs in a working world where no one really cares for them as persons . . . . The high rate of personal and social maladjustment found among social isolates in our large cities testifies to the intensity of the strain under which these people live."[1] The longer professional helpers and volunteers are on the job, the less they self-disclose. Slowly, a light seems to go out in their eyes. The deadening effect of mindless, sterile role conformity by helpers and the inevitable effect of trying to hide their feelings of frustration, anger, and inadequacy should not be minimized. "We are discovering, and soon will demonstrate with more rigorous scientific proofs, that one of the reasons why people fail to grow, why they fail to fulfill many of their potentialities as persons, why they frequently fall ill, is because their daily mode of existence among people is characterized by impersonality, by playing roles, by self manipulation and manipulation of others."[2]

Inability to find a way to relieve the incipient stress leads to *burnout*—the syndrome of *emotional exhaustion and cynicism that occurs after long hours of physical and psychological strain.*

21

To burn out may mean that a helper will become an alcoholic, a drug addict, or mentally ill or even commit suicide.

Definitions

What does burnout mean? Dictionary definitions say that it means failing, wearing out, and becoming exhausted from excessive demands on our energy, strength, and resources. After studying several human service organizations, Cary Cherniss defined burnout as psychological withdrawal from work in response to excessive stress or dissatisfaction with job-related activities.[3] This is not much different from Christina Maslach's observation that burnout is the loss of concern for the people with whom one is working in response to stress.[4] Berkeley Planning Associates defined it in terms of the extent to which helpers have become separated or withdrawn from the original meaning or purpose of their work, the degree to which they are alienated from clients, coworkers, and the agency.[5] All of these definitions were poetically and cogently summarized by Herbert Freudenberger: "Under the strain of living in our complex world, people's inner resources are consumed as if by fire, leaving a great emptiness inside, although their outer shells may be more or less unchanged."[6]

Myths and Stereotypes

It is ironical and sad that professional helpers—individuals trained to diagnose and prescribe for others—often behave in unnecessarily stressful ways. As a whole, human service personnel pay little attention to their own burning out. Furthermore, they spend less time with burned-out clients and, when counseling them, seem to have little to say. Most helpers fight the thought of burnout. Paraphrasing Emily Mumford and James Skipper: Without being aware of how much they demand of themselves, such persons can experience a disturbing sense of personal discomfort when they face the [burned-out client]. [Burnout] is a painful reminder of the realistic limits of the science of [helping] and the skills of the [social] professional, as well as a reminder of human mortality.[7] Professional helpers, contrary to many of their wishes, are but mortal beings. Without assistance, they can neither fly through the air nor walk on top of water.

Yet, there are ample examples of helpers who believe that they must be congruent and in control of themselves at all times. Clients, they think, may be incongruent and out of control, but not them. Some helpers even believe that assisting others to self-actualize is enough reward to keep themselves going. This kind of vicarious identification with the successes of others is hardly enough gratification over the long run. Then there are helpers who believe that they must give most of their time to helping others and virtually none to helping their own families and themselves. I call this the old "show must go on" attitude, even at the expense of the helper's own health and happiness. Finally, there are helpers who believe that if they do their jobs well, then they always will be appreciated and adequately rewarded.

The stereotype of the most effective helper being the person who pushes his or her own needs into the background is the fuel that when ignited burns up the helper's energies and dreams. Within the helping professions, there is a tendency to minimize the importance of *self-love.* In Aristotle's time, it was generally accepted that we should love our best friend, and our best friend is someone who wishes for our well-being.[8] This is the kind of self-love a person should feel in his or her own behalf. Only if we have strong positive feelings for ourselves are we then able to have these feelings for other people. However, helpers who gratify their appetites and emotions in self-destructive ways lack the qualities necessary for assisting others to show restraint.

Another myth is that burnout will disappear if we ignore it. This is an unfortunate belief because burnout is not a condition that gets better by being ignored. The person burning out may be irritable, angry, resistant to change, or listless. Fatigue is a frequent symptom that many individuals experience because of a painful erosion of professional confidence. Other social symptoms include: high resistance to going to work every day, a sense of failure, guilt and blame, frequent clock-watching, dread of contact with clients, avoiding discussions of work with colleagues, reverting to rules and regulations, and self-preoccupation.

Sociopsychological disorders are not less real or less painful than physical injuries. In fact, there are many well-documented physical reactions to psychological stress, including migraine headaches, nausea, belching, diarrhea, dryness of the mouth, excessive salivation, heartburn, ulcers, asthma, and rhinitis.

Burnout in the helping professions is especially high and the reasons are obvious. Dealing with other people's problems on a continuous basis is draining—emotionally and physically. This is compounded by the fact that in all helping situations, there are circumstances beyond the helper's control. It takes an extremely well-adjusted individual to be able to distinguish between failure to help a client achieve a certain goal and failure as a helper. The end result may not be what either the helper or the client wants.

> Certainly we always try to eliminate suffering and especially pain. But it is not the task of therapy merely to reduce mental and physical suffering. One may be inclined to do this because one assumes that the elimination of suffering is an essential or even *the* essential drive of man, as psychoanalysis proclaims in the pleasure principle. But placing this in the foreground would often *not* help the patient. The idea of the pleasure principle, particularly when applied to normal life, overlooks the enormous significance of tension for self-realization in its highest forms. Pleasure, in the sense relief from tension, may be a necessary respite. But it is a phenomenon of standstill. One can achieve the right attitude toward the problem of the elimination of suffering in patients and in normal individuals only if one considers its significance for self-realization and its relationship to the value of health. If the patient is to make the choice we have mentioned, he may still suffer but may *no longer feel sick*, i.e. though somewhat disordered and stricken by a certain anxiety. . . . [9]

Finally, it is important for helpers not to delude themselves into thinking that they can change clients. M. Esther Harding was correct: "We cannot change anyone else; we can change only ourselves, and then usually only when the elements that are in need of reform have become conscious through their reflection in someone else."[10] Professional helpers and volunteers are fighting a battle of credibility on at least three fronts: (1) against the pressure of society for 100 percent success, (2) against the needs of clients for 100 percent success, and (3) against their own internal pressure for 100 percent success. Unlike television and movie stereotypes, the helping professions consist of hazardous, basically nonglamorous jobs. The financial rewards for most helpers are few and the personal risks are great. Little wonder, then, that burnout in the helping professions is quite high.

Those Who Are Affected

Although no job is immune from burnout, some produce more stress than others. Teachers, welfare workers, police officers, child-care workers, psychologists, counselors, and other human service professionals are high on the list of persons who have a great probability of burning out, but social agency professions are not alone. Business executives, physicians, nurses, secretaries, salespersons, air traffic controllers, and farmers also have high burnout rates.

A 1979 study of six occupations by the American Academy of Family Physicians concluded that 81 percent of the business respondents, 62 percent of the teachers and secretaries, 44 percent of the garment workers, and 38 percent of the farmers experienced extreme stress in their jobs.[11] Severe stress leads to absenteeism. The financial significance of these and other data is seen in the following:

1. In 1980 the Bureau of Labor Statistics reported that Americans lost 3.3 percent of work hours through absenteeism.
2. On any given day, one out of three workers has called in sick because of job-related stress.
3. The National Association of Mental Health estimates that stress disorders cost organizations $17 billion to $25 billion each year in lost performance and health benefit payments.

Studies of teachers and child-care workers provide in-depth analyses of burnout. In an article entitled "The Big Click," Robert Scrivens noted that teachers who have worked for more than a decade are the most likely ones to burn out.[12] The psychological conditions that trigger burnout are related to the way most young teachers begin their careers—inspired, idealistic, and energetic. The system they seek to change has an uncanny way of wearing the neophytes down and changing them. Suddenly, or so it often seems, the Don Quixotes of education become cynical people with little energy or resolve to change "the system." Inadequate pay has much to do with them burning out, but it is not the sole reason as many people believe.

Despite the fact that persons entering teaching have fairly real-istic notions about their salary potential, low salaries produce stress, but so too do violence on school premises and changing societal values. Teachers are greatly affected by life-style changes. Within the past twenty years, American life-styles have undergone considerable change. Consequently, it is understandable that teach-ers (and other human service professionals) are confused about the behavior they are to model and community values they are to en-force. The United States Supreme Court does not clarify these is-sues; rather, recent rulings have added further confusion.

Child-care workers burn out for the same reasons that human service workers in other low status fields burn out: low pay, long hours, inadequate fringe benefits, and high client-to-worker ra-tios.[13] With little chance for job advancement, most child-care workers frequently switch jobs in order to enhance their salaries by a few more pennies an hour. In short, being underpaid and overworked is a stressful condition. Perhaps in the end, child-care workers burn out for the same reason that the teachers burn out: there is little emotional compensation for their demanding jobs.

In *Staff Burnout,* Cary Cherniss gave four reasons why burn-out is an important issue in human services.[14] First, it negatively affects a staff's team morale and individual well-being. Second, it negatively affects the quality of client care. Third, it impacts nega-tively on administrative functioning. Fourth, it is an important is-sue even if it is not experienced by agency personnel; clients are likely to have burned out. By now it should be clear that the issue of burnout has more than economic dimensions. Sure, lost wages and agency funds are important considerations. However, of fore-most consideration are the wasted human lives. Money can be re-placed, but human beings are not replaceable. We can get others to do their jobs, but we cannot replace them because of the unique-ness of each person.

But we are not talking about isolated individuals who suffer burnout in the solitude of themselves. On the contrary, burnout affects the significant other persons of the individuals afflicted with it. Increased urbanization and agency mechanization have meant a decline in community life and the absence of meaningful social activities for helpers. Each year more helpers find themselves trapped in an impersonal technostructure in which their desires to meet, exchange ideas, and develop close relationships are unful- · filled.

Most social institutions seem to have lost their ability to provide staff members with ways of finding these satisfactions. Traditional human service organizations are as a whole not providing the mechanisms for closeness. If the growing number of people attending human relations workshops is a valid indication, then there is a tremendous hunger for intimacy, relatedness, care, affection, and understanding that our institutions of employment, religion, and family are not providing.

Erich Fromm called attention to the need of people to develop wholesome personalities through socialization.[15] The personality, Fromm noted, is shaped by the way in which persons relate to each other, and this relationship is determined by the socioeconomic and political structure of a nation. In most instances, individual needs are not being satisfied. There is a conflict between human needs and social structure. The middle-class life for most helpers, while satisfying basic material needs, leaves most workers with a feeling of intense personal or professional emptiness.

The clients are also unfulfilled. Many clients utilizing social agency services have unmet basic survival needs as well as higher level needs. Increased mobility compounds this situation. Mobility detaches both helpers and clients from permanent, significant collegial relationships. Occupational specialization adds to this detachment because it forces people to follow their jobs instead of friends. Thus, human service workers and their clients have become organization men and women.

David Riesman called the organization men and women the "other-directed"—unable to distinguish thoughts from feelings and unable to express feelings even when recognizing them.[16] This is a common characteristic of people who burn out. Today, more than thirty years after Riesman wrote *The Lonely Crowd*, the organization people are still with us, most of them unable to distinguish between what they want and what they ought to want. Decisions of this nature are left to their supervisors. The other-directed helpers are attuned to the attitudes and opinions of others and they have insatiable psychological needs for success. They find fulfillment only when they are praised by their significant others. It is not unusual to hear burned-out helpers lament, "I'm not appreciated." In many instances they become generally passive, indecisive, and low in self-esteem.

Erich Fromm's conception of the typical agency person, the "marketer," is similar to Riesman's other-directed person.[17] Helpers fitting the marketer category derive their self-esteem from their value of salability as a commodity or investment (i.e. "I am what I do"). At some point in their lives, the responsibility of freedom becomes too frightening for them, so they live by conforming to social pressures and seeking approval from others. In spite of economic or professional success, there is a sense of emptiness among them. They feel impotent within their bureaucratic organizations and ultimately they drop out of meaningful agency relationships. In sociopsychological terms, they become *alienated* — they lose touch with themselves and join the "lonely crowd."

But I do not wish to dismiss too quickly the "burden" that many helpers carry. Helpers who burn out imagine themselves as somehow being responsible for the decisions of their clients. Thus anguish, abandonment, and despair are natural responses to these unrealistic societal responsibilities. Most individuals who accept this type of responsibility cannot help but feel a profound sense of guilt (even anxiety) when they choose destinies for others. "Who can then prove that I am the proper person to impose, by my own choice, my conception of man upon mankind?" Sartre asked. "If a voice speaks to me, it is still I myself who must decide whether the voice is or is not that of an angel."[18] Burning out is sometimes the result of finding out that we hear neither angels nor devils, only human voices.

An important theme of helping, one which most helpers can identify with and find comfort in, is the notion that we are many people — some good, some bad. "The world is made up of people, but the people of the world forget this. It is hard to believe that, like ourselves, other people are born of women, reared by parents, teased by brothers, . . . consoled by wives, . . . flattered by grandchildren, and buried by parsons and priests with the blessing of the church and the tears of those left behind. . . . It is easier to speak of fate, and destiny, and waves of the future than to see the ways we determine our own fate, right now and in the immediate past and future."[19]

Special Programs

There are numerous programs designed to prepare people to cope with burnout. Once we become aware of burnout and burned-out individuals, then the road to recovery, which is personal for each of us, becomes more than mere theory or wishes. There are many recommendations that anyone can follow to stop the burnout syndrome.

Thomas McGaffey states that any organization planning for stress disorder prevention must consider individual responses to adjustive demands.[20] The complex array of disorders arising from stress clearly requires that administrators be aware of the many types of prevention programs. There is a newly evolving management control system for dealing with employee stress called the Employee Assistance Program (EAP). The EAP is a stress-intervention program that can serve as an effective base for developing a comprehensive system for preventing and abating organizational stress or burnout.

The basic activity upon which the EAP is built is the *performance contract*, which stipulates that the employee promises performance and reliability in return for the benefits provided by the organization, including pay, opportunity for advancement, and fringe benefits. The basic elements of the EAP are as follows:

1. A policy statement outlining the elements of the performance contract, specifically identifying the view that many performance problems are due to factors out of control of the individual, that the organization will not accept continued poor performance and absenteeism, but that it will assist the employee with obtaining assistance with the causal problem.
2. In union organizations, an endorsement by the union of the program and its benefits to employees.
3. Definite work performance standards that are clearly defined. Unsatisfactory performance will be brought to the attention of the employee also.
4. The recognition that performance problems will have a range of causes and that performance may be affected by any one of these factors or combinations of them.

5. A diagnostic and referral intake resource that is professionally competent to make a definitive and accurate referral to the appropriate help-providing agency.
6. The availability of a comprehensive health model treatment system that can respond to the diagnosed problem. This system may be a single agency or a combination of community treatment resources.
7. The alignment of the insurance benefits available to the employees so that treatment may be covered for all the disorders included in the EAP system.
8. A system of evaluation to gauge the impact of EAP and its effectiveness.[21]

It is evident that an agency considering instituting the EAP should be aware that it is a cost factor not to be taken lightly. However, studies of these programs indicate that the initial costs are more than offset by the decrease in absenteeism, health costs, and indemnity costs. Even so, the initial starting costs are prohibitive in many human service organizations like schools, mental health institutions, day-care centers, and groupwork agencies. Administrators in public institutions are painfully aware that the public tends to be leary of helping organizations themselves being in need of help. Furthermore, there is seldom enough money to start new programs, especially those benefiting employees. Going to the community to ask for more money for this type of program is fraught with public relations problems. Assuming that funds are secured, there must be a real commitment on the part of management to make an EAP program successful.

In a recent *Reader's Digest* article, it was reported that the most frequent methods for coping with job stress were overeating, overdrinking, smoking, drug use, and daydreaming.[22] Often, people in the crisis stage of burnout develop a *flight* response. For example, women will get pregnant so they will not have to work outside their homes. If untreated, burnout can reach the stage where an individual's life deteriorates to the point of being endangered. Slightly less dramatic but equally terminal outcomes of burnout are chemical abuse, heart disease, and mental illness.

Human service professionals are just beginning to tackle the problem of overcoming public apathy, organization inertia, and individual neglect, which not only provides the fuel but also lights the flames of burnout. A good night's sleep or a few extra dollars will not stop the growth of a long-festering burnout. The more effective programs are comprehensive, not superficial remedies.

The Northwest Staff Development Center (NSDC), a federally funded teacher center, has developed a program to address the issue of teacher and administrator stress and burnout. The NSDC workshops have four goals: (1) to reduce the isolation that many school personnel experience; (2) to identify the sources of job-related stress; (3) to identify professional strengths and successful work experiences that participants can draw on to increase their job satisfaction; and (4) to formulate plans to prevent or alleviate stress. A typical NSDC workshop contains the following basic components: (1) an opening series of questions to raise several key issues that will be developed in later sessions; (2) a review of the workshop's goals and assumptions and a discussion of several possible blocks to participants' self-awareness and problem solving; (3) an exercise to break down barriers between participants and to generate discussion of several sensitive stress-related issues; (4) an assessment of each participant's strengths and weaknesses; and (5) a brief presentation of theory about stress.[23]

Cherniss outlines the following points for agency directors concerned about preventing and abating staff burnout:[24]

Staff Development

- Reduce demands workers impose on themselves by encouraging them to adopt more realistic goals.
- Encourage workers to adopt new goals that might provide alternative sources of gratification.
- Help workers develop and use monitoring and feedback mechanisms sensitive to short-term gains.
- Provide frequent opportunities for in-service training designed to increase role effectiveness.
- Teach staff coping strategies such as time study and management techniques.
- Orient new staff by providing them with a booklet that realistically describes typical frustrations and difficulties that occur in the job.
- Provide periodic "burnout checkups" for all staff.

- Provide work-focused counseling or consultation to staff who are experiencing high levels of stress in their jobs.
- Encourage the development of support groups and/or resource exchange networks.

Job and Role Structures

- Limit number of clients for whom staff are responsible at any one time.
- Spread the most difficult and unrewarding work among all staff, and require staff to work in more than one role and program.
- Arrange each day so that the rewarding and unrewarding activities alternate.
- Structure roles in ways that allow workers to take "time-outs" whenever necessary.
- Use auxiliary personnel (e.g. volunteers) to provide other staff with opportunities for time-outs.
- Encourage workers to take frequent vacations and give short notice only if necessary.
- Limit the number of hours that a staff person works.
- Do not discourage part-time employment.
- Give every staff member the opportunity to create new programs.
- Build in career ladders for all staff.

Management Development

- Create management training and development programs for current and potential supervisory personnel, emphasizing those aspects of the role that administrators have most difficulty with.
- Create monitoring systems for supervisory personnel, such as staff surveys, and give supervisory personnel regular feedback on their performance.
- Monitor role strain in supervisory personnel, and intervene when strain becomes excessive.

Problem-Solving and Decision-Making

- Create formal mechanisms for group and organizational problem solving and conflict resolution.
- Provide training in conflict resolution and group problem solving for all staff.
- Maximize staff autonomy and participation in decision making.

Agency Goals

- Make goals as clear and consistent as possible. Develop a strong, distinctive, guiding philosophy.
- Make education and research a major focus of the program.
- Share responsibility for care and treatment with the client, the client's family, and the community.[24]

Human service agencies are beginning to realize that it is not enough to help clients, but they must also help their staffs. Though the agencies may offer help to burnout victims, that offer must first be accepted. With or without agency help, there are things each individual can do to help himself or herself. Now, we will look at some specific self-help activities.

Techniques and Tips

There are several ways for people to avoid job burnout. Since the job may be the source of burnout, some people should put distance between themselves and their jobs. They should not set themselves up for additional failure by establishing unattainable career goals. It is both counterproductive and stressful for workaholics to ignore leisure-time activities. Everyone should have outside activities and interests. The pursuit of almost any nonagency recreational project can reduce stress. Regular exercise is one of the best ways to avoid burnout fatigue, but care should be taken not to overdo it. Breaking the daily routine of work may initially be stressful if an individual has forgotten how to relax.

Most helpers do not do enough for themselves. Prolonged stress can affect an individual's personal life away from work. It can make people unhappy with their loved ones, unable to be happy during "free" times, and leave them listless and angry. Each of us must learn to pay attention to physical symptoms, to put career goals in proper perspective, and to understand the nature of burnout. Only then can we control our job, rather than allowing it to control us.

Numerous researchers have dealt with ways to combat burnout. First, we must avoid false cures. Many people use the defense mechanism of *denial* as a way of avoiding pain. In order to solve a problem, we must acknowledge that there is something threatening our well-being. Denial is not always bad, but once it becomes obsessive and crosses over the pain threshold into dulling and deadening our senses, it works against us. If we continue to deaden ourselves, we create havoc in our lives; the problem only gets worse. Camouflage does not make the burnout go away. No matter what form it takes, denial does not solve problems. Another form of denial is to become other-directed. We can suspend our own motivating forces and abdicate our responsibility by acquiescing to the will of others. When we become other-directed, we deny our own importance and mold ourselves according to externally imposed standards.

There are two reliable cures for burnout: closeness and being inner-directed. Before we can achieve closeness with others, we have to achieve it with ourselves. People who burn out seldom spend enough time with themselves in a constructive manner. Closeness is anywhere and with anyone we choose. Inner-directedness is not being selfish. Rather, it is taking time out for one's own self. The purpose, of course, is to do things that are good for our renewal.

People in the helping professions should watch for signs of burnout even when things appear to be going well. It is too easy for helpers to become martyrs who defy their own gratification. We should watch for tiredness before it becomes extreme exhaustion. Nor should we fall into the trap of believing ourselves to be superhumans who do not require rest. Attention should be paid to physical symptoms such as colds or nagging pains in the back. Also, we should monitor ourselves for shifts in attitude, especially towards self-doubt or pity.

People who choose to enter relatively low-paying helping professions usually have a sense of altruistic mission. They are compassionate and caring, which makes them especially vulnerable to the excessive demands that are made on them. Unless the worker remains aware of his or her vulnerability, it is likely burnout will occur. Above all else, we must watch for signs of growing rigid, increasing negativism, and cynicism. Like the Chinese Yin and Yang, we must keep the world in balance.

There are specific ways that people in the helping professions can stop themselves from falling victim to burnout. Stephen Valle recommends the following self-help for counselors: (1) recognize the symptoms, (2) learn to ask for help, (3) be aware of your limitations, (4) maintain self-discipline, (5) take time-outs,* (6) diversify responsibilities, (7) do not set unrealistic job expectations, (8) identify goals and carefully evaluate them, and (9) seek opportunities for professional and personal growth.[25]

Angelo Boy and Gerald Pine list the following recommendations for identifying professional goals that will enable counselors to handle increasing role demands: (1) spend the major portion of the working day counseling clients; (2) know the authentic needs of clients; (3) carefully select an organization to be associated with; (4) associate with committed, concerned colleagues; (5) develop a sense of organizational involvement; (6) become committed to a theory of counseling; (7) engage in self-assessment; (8) periodically examine the counseling role; and (9) maintain an attitude of hope.[26] To this list I would add, Maintain a sense of humor.

Dorothy Moe—an elementary teacher who experienced burnout, quit teaching, and returned to the classroom two years later—devised a sixteen-point plan for preventing burnout: (1) exercise daily, (2) leave teaching at school, (3) develop a hobby, (4) get plenty of sleep, (5) don't feel guilty because you haven't lived up to your ideal of the perfect teacher, (6) keep a diary of the wacky things the kids do, say, and write on their papers, (7) don't worry, (8) learn to say no, (9) be good to yourself, (10) always have something to look forward to, (11) do something in your spare time that you have always dreamed of doing, (12) keep learning, (13) travel, (14) don't schedule all your leisure hours, (15) set realistic

---

*Time-outs are structured breaks during the day when a counselor puts distance between himself or herself and emotional encounters.

goals for yourself, and (16) take a sabbatical or a leave of absence.[27]

In conclusion, there are as many ways to prevent and stop burnout as there are people who experience it. However, in reviewing the articles presented, some recommendations appear over and over again. As individuals, there are a number of things that we can and must do to help ourselves. *Each of us should devise our own plan to prevent or abate burnout.* As is often the case, it is easier to get the medicine than compliance. Too many of us pause and hesitate, often until it is too late. Being a well-rounded person relieves the stress. The task is to become a well-rounded person. For some helpers, their priorities get distracted or poorly set and burnout closes the debate over which action will prevent it.

Effective personnel intervention in a burnout situation may require modifying one's job description or altering one's relationship with clients, colleagues, subordinates, and supervisors. In other instances, it may mean returning to school to obtain better credentials or taking a leave to sort things out. It may mean changing one's off-duty activities or even changing one's job. In essence, it means reducing the stress and taking care of oneself. The remaining chapters will focus on stress-related problems and recommendations for change.

EXERCISE DRILL

The Change Scale[28]

Life Event	Mean Value
1. Death of a spouse	100
2. Divorce	73
3. Marital separation	65
4. Jail term	63
5. Death of close family member	63
6. Personal injury or illness	53
7. Marriage	50

If your total score on the Change Scale is 600 points, you are probably in a major crisis and possibly out of control. If you are between 300–500 points you may want to slow down a bit. If you are 100–200, you may be going a little too slow and need to add some excitement or challenge to your life. A score of 200–300 is about right for most people.

8. Fired at work	47	
9. Marital reconciliation	45	
10. Retirement	45	
11. Change in health of family member	44	
12. Pregnancy	40	
13. Sex difficulties	39	
14. Gain of new family member	39	
15. Business readjustments	39	
16. Change in financial state	38	
17. Death of close friend	37	
18. Change to different line of work	36	
19. Change in number of arguments with spouse	35	
20. Mortgage over $10,000	31	
21. Foreclosure of mortgage or loan	30	
22. Change in responsibilities at work	29	
23. Son or daughter leaving home	29	
24. Trouble with in-laws	29	
25. Outstanding personal achievement	28	
26. Wife begin or stop work	26	
27. Begin or end school	26	
28. Change in living conditions	25	
29. Revision of personal habits	24	
30. Trouble with boss	23	
31. Change in work hours or conditions	20	
32. Change in residence	20	
33. Change in schools	20	
34. Change in recreation	19	
35. Change in church activities	19	
36. Change in social activities	18	
37. Mortgage or loan less than $10,000	17	
38. Change in sleeping habits	16	
39. Change in number of family get-togethers	15	TOTAL
40. Change in eating habits	15	POINTS
41. Vacation	13	
42. Christmas	12	
43. Minor violations of the law	11	

REFERENCES

1. Kaplan, L.: *Foundations of Human Behavior.* New York: Harper & Row, 1965, p. 200.

2. Episcopal Church: *Basic Reader in Human Relations Training, Part II.* New York: Service to Dioceses, 1970, p. 28.

3. Cherniss, C.: *Professional Burnout in Human Service Organizations.* New York: Praeger, 1968, p. 16.

4. Maslach, C.: Burned-out. *Human Behavior, 519*:16–22, 1976.

5. Berkeley Planning Associates: "Project Management and Worker Burnout." Unpublished report, 1977.

6. Freudenberger, H.J.: *Burn-Out: The High Cost of Achievement.* New York: Doubleday, 1980, p. xv.

7. Mumford, E., and Skipper, J.K., Jr.: *Sociology in Hospital Care.* New York: Harper & Row, 1967, p. 203.

8. Aristotle: *Nicomachean Ethics.* Translated by Martin Ostwald. New York: Bobbs–Merrill, 1963, p. 20.

9. Goldstein, K.: Health as value. In Maslow, A.H. (Ed.): *New Knowledge in Values.* Chicago: Henry Regnery, 1959, p. 182.

10. Harding, M.E.: *The "I" and the "Not-I."* Princeton: Princeton University Press, 1965, p. 75.

11. Muse, J.: Survival of stressed teachers. *National Educational Association Instruction and Professional Development.* Washington, D.C.: NEA, 1979, p. 5.

12. Scrivens, R.: The big click. *Today's Education, 68*:14, 1979.

13. Whitebook, M., Howes, C., Darrah, R., and Friedman, J.: Who's minding the child care workers?: A look at staff burn-out. *Children Today, 10:* 2-6, 1981.

14. Cherniss, C.: *Staff Burnout.* Beverly Hills: Sage, 1980, p. 28.

15. Fromm, E.: *The Sane Society.* New York: Fawcett, 1968, p. 19.

16. Riesman, D.: *The Lonely Crowd: A Study of Changing American Character.* New Haven: Yale University Press, 1950.

17. Fromm, E.: *Man for Himself: An Inquiry into the Psychology of Ethics.* New York: Fawcett, 1967.

18. Jean-Paul Sartre. Quoted in Kaufman, W.A. (Ed.): *Existentialism from Dosteovsky to Sartre.* New York: Meridian Books, 1965, p. 293.

19. Menninger, K.: *Love Against Hate.* New York: Harcourt, Brace, 1942, p. 114.

20. McGaffey, T.N.: New horizons in organizational stress prevention approaches. *Personnel Administrator, 23:*26, 1978.

21. Ibid., p. 28.

22. Veninga, R.L., and Spradley, J.P.: "How to Cope with Job Burnout." *Reader's Digest*, December, 1981, p. 110.

23. Sparks, D.: A teacher center tackles the issue. *Today's Education, 68*: 43, 1979.

24. Cherniss, *Staff Burnout,* pp. 184–185.

25. Valle, S.K.: Burn-out: Occupational hazard for counselors. *Alcohol Health and Research World, 5*:13–14, 1980.

26. Boy, A.V., and Pine, G.J.: "Avoiding Counselor Burnout Through Role Reversal." *Reader's Digest,* January, 1981, p. 87.

27. Moe, D.: A prescription. *Today's Education, 68*:51, 1979.
28. Tubesing, D.A.: *Stress Skills*. Oakbrook, Il.: Whole Person Associates, 1979, p. 13. Based on Holmes, T.H., and Rahe, R.J.: The social readjustment rating scale. *Journal of Psychosomatic Research, 12*:213–218, 1967.

Chapter 3
WOMEN

FROM an historical perspective it is evident that capitalism, through its wage-labor system, introduced an important distinction between the sexes: men began to work for wages outside their homes, while women continued to work within their homes without wages. Despite mechanical aids altering the way women worked, this did almost nothing to change the type of work assigned to women (e.g. domestic, family maintenance, reproduction, and the socialization of children). The so-called "women's work" continued to be seen as natural functions and instinctive and of little importance when compared with "men's work." The downgrading of women's work has been a foremost cause of current status problems of women. Even when pre-1970 women supplemented their families' income through work at home by taking in boarders, laundry, or children, for example, their efforts continued to go unheralded; it was viewed as a part of their routine household chores.

Until World War II, most married women living with their husbands worked outside their homes only if they were extremely poor or if a hardship was experienced, such as the husband being unable to work or pay the bills. Middle-class and upper-class mothers were expected to remain at home with their children, and if they did not their employment meant that their husbands were inadequate in some respect, and this was a blow to their self-esteem and that of their families.

Numerous rationalizations were used by employers for paying women less, but the major reason was quite simple: it was profitable. Not only were women forced to accept underemployment, seasonal employment, and tedious tasks, but they were also viewed as being expendable during periods of economic recession. Excluded from most skilled jobs and the opportunity to learn trades, women had few choices but to accept low wages and poor working conditions. As a result of these conditions, countless women preferred housework, especially since they had to do it anyway, even those who worked outside their homes. Little has changed since 1970. The issue is not women but, instead, sexism.

Definitions

Sexism is the process of assigning life roles according to gender. This system fosters sex-related roles that usually relegate men to positions of authority in government, industry, education, science, and business.[1] Although sometimes used only in reference to prejudice against females, sexism means any stereotyping resulting in arbitrary discrimination against females or males.

Sexism is an integral part of our society. It is an insidious infestation hidden in the very core of our lives, and it has a cumulative effect upon all of our societal functions that is reflected in our life-styles, economic institutions, religious doctrines, and personal relations. It is perpetuated and supported by the manner in which males and females are socialized. The basic institutions of socialization are education and the family. Sexism begins in the family. The behaviors associated with sexism are so deeply ingrained into our minds that sexist behavior is generally unconscious. Both men and women practice sexism in their daily behavior by means of speech, dress, attitudes, and goals.

Sexism respects neither race nor color nor culture. It can be compared with racism in that it identifies a portion of the population and designates them different and, therefore, inferior. Sexism, like racism, involves the combination of power and prejudice. The power originally assumed by men was generally ascribed to them because of their greater physical strength and speed needed as hunters and warriors in early civilizations. The male dominance and female passiveness has remained in cultural, institutional, and individual practices even though technological advancement has negated strength and speed as required factors of dominance.

Both sexism and racism have been documented throughout history, but racism has received more attention in the news media; consequently, minority males have gained more in the area of social justice. For example, although companies that have contracts with the federal government are bound by law to hire and promote regardless of race and sex, these companies have until recently done a better job of locating, hiring, and integrating minority males into their work force. This is not to suggest that the racial struggle has been won, but only to note priorities. In addition, it should be noted that sexism exists within racism, thus becoming a double problem for minority women.

Myths and Stereotypes

John Stuart Mill regarded women as a subject class. However, he recognized that the state of female bondage in at least one respect was a refinement over that of the black slave; each man wants his woman to be "not a forced slave, but a willing one; not a slave, merely, but a favorite." In "The Subjection of Women," he emphasized that subtle and pervasive social conditioning is the means by which women are prepared to accede to roles as the servants of men.[2]

Sigmund Freud was critical of Mill's study of women, believing that it gave insufficient consideration to what Freud construed to be inborn temperamental differences between the sexes. Freud said, "Despite my thirty years in research into the feminine soul, I have not yet been able to answer . . . the great question that has never been answered: What does a woman want?"[3]

One of the answers that those active in contemporary women's liberation movements would give is cessation of the stereotypes of female status—the casual acceptance that women are less than human. Simone de Beauvoir, one of the intellectual stalwarts of the women's equality movement, wrote in *The Second Sex* that society, being codified by men, decrees that the female is inferior. Betty Friedan, in her 1963 best-seller, *The Feminine Mystique,* documented the problems of middle-class housewives and observed that the American society seems bent upon persuading the housewife that all that is requisite for the fulfillment of those of her gender can be found in the cleaning, cooking, and child-rearing climate of the home. John Stuart Mill observed: "When we consider the positive evil caused to the disqualified half of the human race by their disqualification—first in the loss of the most inspiring and elevating kind of personal enjoyment, and next in the weariness, disappointment, and profound dissatisfaction with life, which are so often the substitute for it—one feels that among all the lessons which men require for carrying the struggle against the inevitable imperfections of their lot on earth, there is no lesson which they more need, than not to add to the evils which nature inflicts, by their jealous and prejudiced restrictions on one another."[4]

Many of the roots of the contemporary women's rights movements stem from the prejudices and frustrations women encounter regularly when they attempt to leave their "designated" role and enter the world of work, research, or study. Psychologically and professionally, many find that established legal principles are not operative in daily practice in the outside world of trade and service. Perhaps the most damaging of all the handicaps a woman faces when she enters that world is the general assumption that a man by his very nature is capable of more than she is and in every respect. The subtle psychological implications of this are reflected in early toys and unwittingly absorbed in childhood. Toys are constructed to imply that boys are activistic and will grow up to create and produce. Girl's toys, on the other hand, cater to a more passive nature and point toward a feminine role meant to nourish and consume.

Further psychological reinforcement for submissiveness is added when females are admonished that having an intellect may, in fact, be a hazard that will discourage proposals of marriage—the only worthy, ultimate goal for women. The effectiveness of this conditioning would tend to be supported by the fact that girls outperform boys in academic work *until* their late teens, when culturally established goals of marriage assume paramount importance, and a degree of reversal occurs.

Despite a fairly pervasive effort over a long period of time to predetermine the role and direction women should take, the results achieved, both past and present, have been far from uniform. Some women are very interested in female quality, some are apathetic, and some stand firmly against it. Kathleen Snow concluded, "Some women confess that their pro-liberation thinking is at odds with their anti-liberation feelings; they have been intellectually persuaded, but their hearts belong to the old order."[5]

Pat Crigler, a psychologist at Northwestern University in Chicago, became very interested in why the active feminist role attracts some women and repels others. Finding no satisfactory answers at hand, she set about querying 750 women in Atlanta and Chicago. Two groups were selected for this study: the liberal National Organization for Women (NOW), and a more conservative organization, the League of Women Voters. Psychologist Crigler reported: "If I were going to say what has the most bearing on why a woman becomes a feminist, my answer would have to be that when there is a girl in the house who is for women's rights, it is the influence of her father."[6]

This study further indicated that the more education the father has, the more likelihood there is that the daughter will be a feminist. Still another significant factor determined by this study is that the higher the educational level in the home, the more likely girls are to believe in equal rights. An only child, it was determined, has a natural impetus toward a role beyond that of the traditional woman. "If you are the only child, you have to try to live up to the expectations of both parents. This means you learn both to sew and to fix the car. You are the confidante of both parents, and you see both sides of the fence. So you pick out the logical position for women, rather than the traditional."[7]

Nonfeminists, the study showed, were likely to be women busy with large families. The more children a woman has, particularly if she does not work outside the home, the more likely it is that she is not going to be in favor of equal rights. From this study, the author concluded that there is considerable difference in perspective between those advocating equal rights and those active in women's liberation. There is a broader philosophical base for current trends than some of the most vocal spokespersons in both the pro and the con fringe areas of women's equality movements would have us believe. Crigler concluded that the term *feminism* is a misnomer for what we are seeing. "It is not women's lib, it is not the battle of the sexes. These are very poor descriptions of an interest in equal rights for all — of everyone striving to be accepted as a person and not be stereotyped."[8]

The rebellion against the stereotypes of female status and against the casual assumption that women are inferior human beings was the impetus for the formation of organizations to dispel such myths. The role of women in the labor and military forces in the World War II era and after that time made attitudes and acts of inequity for women of more than theoretical concern to those who were subjected to them. The increased number of women who did enter the work force was an important element in the institution and growth of the feminist movement of the 1960s and 1970s.

Commenting on the prevailing stereotype of a wife's role, Judy Syfers noted that most men say, " 'I want a wife who will take care of my physical needs . . . keep my house clean . . . keep my clothes clean, ironed, and replaced when need be . . . take care of the details of my social life . . . remain sexually faithful . . . understand that my sexual needs may entail more than strict adherence to monogamy.' My God, who wouldn't want a wife?"[9] In a sympathetic vein, David Riesman mused: "I think what I would ideally like to see in our society is that sex become an ascribed rather than an achieved status. That one is simply born a girl or a boy and that's it. And no worry about an activity's de-feminizing or emasculating one."[10] Riesman will not get his wish if the prediction that the family of the future will remain deeply ingrained in institutions influencing employment, income maintenance, marriage, sex relations, divorce, and mental health comes true.

Just as white males used paternalism to keep blacks in "their place" during slavery, chivalry is being used to keep women in their place today. The old masculinist places women on a pedestal so that he knows where they are at all times. Women in the world of work frequently step down from their pedestals. When Garda Bowman interviewed business executives, she uncovered a great deal of hostility toward female executives. Most of the males queried felt that women were "temperamentally unfit for management."[11] Bowman pointed out that when male executives became angry and had outbursts of temper, they were admired by other males for their manly anger; but when women executives displayed the same behavior, they were considered emotionally unstable.

"Nowhere is this disparity between reality and myth as the foundation for social policy more evident than in regard to the large-scale movement of women into the labor force—a phenomenon that could have consequences of immense magnitude for the nation. Its effects on the economy, on the labor market, on family welfare, and on community life are already apparent. It has become both an aspect of change and a prime mover for further change. Yet, in our failure to take account of this occurrence may be the cause of hardship and inequity for increasing numbers of people, and the potential for considerable social unrest."[12]

While economic factors certainly play a key role in the decision of many women to join the work force, this is not (contrary to popular notion) the only explanation. Women have been employed in most human service agencies long before salaries were improved. Perhaps the least persuasive reason attributes the current increase in women's employment to the women's liberation movement. Some critics even say feminists are driving women out of the home. Another explanation is that women are bored because modern appliances make housework so easy, that women have difficulty finding enough housework to fill the time that their mothers and grandmothers spent keeping house. There is little evidence to support either of these subjective views. A more reasonable view attributes the increase in out-of-home employed women to the lowered birth rate, the increase in women's education, longer life expectancy, the rising divorce rate, and rising expectations about what constitutes a good life.

Single women and women who are the sole supporters of their families have always worked. Therefore, their increased participation rates should come as no real surprise. However, married women, especially mothers of small children, are the ones whose presence needs an explanation. Today's mothers generally have fewer children than their grandmothers, they have a longer life expectancy after their children are grown, and they have invested more in their own education. A married mother may want her children to have more than she had and may find that her husband's salary is not enough to provide it. It may also be that one paycheck does not go far enough toward achieving the life-style to which Americans have been encouraged to aspire. In any case, the married woman's major impetus appears to be a desire to earn money she feels she *needs*, instead of any desire to actualize herself as a liberated feminist or to fill up empty hours.[13]

One could argue that women have less access to education than men and, therefore, are confined to lower-paying jobs. This, however, is not supported by evidence. According to recent United States Department of Labor statistics, the average female worker is as well educated as the average male worker—both having completed a median of 12.6 years of schooling. The sad fact of the matter is that on the whole, women with college degrees earn less than men with an eighth-grade education. In 1979, the woman worker with a college degree earned a median salary of $13,430, while the male worker with only an eighth-grade education earned a median salary of $14,475.

The fact that statistics confirm women are earning much less than men and are still, for the most part, entering a narrow range of occupations seems to support the view that our social attitudes and values about what is and is not appropriate behavior for men and women are hard to alter. Even in the helping professions, women are underrepresented in administrative positions. As long as girls are encouraged to pursue "feminine" interests and boys encouraged to pursue "masculine" interests, the status quo will be reinforced—some jobs will be seen as suitable for males and others for females.

Those Who Are Affected

Statistics reveal that between 1970 and 1978, the number of female workers increased from nearly 32 million to 42 million (about 1.5 times more than the increase in the number of male workers). As a result, there were about seven female workers in 1978 for every ten male workers—an increase of one female worker per ten male workers over the 1970 ratio. The increases occurred among women of all ages, but they were especially pronounced for women under 45 years of age. The number of women 16 to 24 years old in the labor force grew by over one-third, while the number of female workers 25 to 34 years old nearly doubled. Both population growth and increased labor force participation played a part in these increases. The labor force participation rate for women age 20 to 24 increased from 58 percent in 1970 to nearly 69 percent in 1978. Women 25 to 34 years old showed an even greater increase, with rates rising from 45 percent to 62 percent during the same period. The movement of the baby-boom generation into these age categories helped account for much of the labor force growth in these age groups.[14]

The increase in the labor force participation rates of women has occurred along with a decline in the participation rates for men. The overall, annual labor force participation rate for women increased from about 43 percent in 1970 to about 50 percent in 1978. However, the annual rate for men declined from about 81 percent to 78 percent for this period. Rising participation rates for women in the face of decreasing rates for men have given women an increasing share of the nation's work force (from 37 percent in 1970 to 41 percent in 1978). The Bureau of the Census projects women to reach 47 percent by 1990. Declines in labor force participation rates have occurred in most age groups for men, whereas women have experienced increasing labor force rates in all age groups under 55 years. The decline of men reflects, in part, the spread and liberalization of pension, disability, and retirement plans as well as changing social attitudes toward work and leisure. The fact that rates for women have risen in the presence of some of these same forces attests to the strength and durability of the movement of women into the labor force.

With this general statistical background, let us now examine some other facts that seem to suggest reasons why participation rates for women are on the rise. Facts provided by the United States Department of Labor's Women's Bureau indicate that:

1. Of the 43 million women workers in the labor force in 1979, the majority work because of economic need. Nearly two-thirds of all women in the labor force in 1979 were single, widowed, divorced, separated, or had husbands whose earnings were less than $10,000 (in 1978).

2. Fifty-three percent of all black women were in the labor force in 1979 (5 million); they accounted for nearly half of all black workers. Forty-seven percent of Spanish-origin women were in the labor force in 1979 (2 million); they accounted for 39 percent of all Spanish-origin workers.

3. The more education a woman has, the greater the likelihood she will seek paid employment. Among women with four or more years of college, about two out of three were in the labor force in 1979.

4. The number of working mothers has increased more than tenfold since the period immediately preceding World War II, while the number of working women more than tripled. Fifty-five percent of mothers with children under 18 years (16.6 million) were in the labor force in 1979; 45 percent of mothers with preschool children were working (6 million).

5. Among all families, about one out of seven was maintained by a woman in 1979, compared with about one out of ten in 1969; 40 percent of black families were maintained by women. Of all women workers, about one out of six maintained a family; about one out of four black women workers maintained a family.

6. Among all poor families, half were maintained by women in 1979; about three out of four poor black families were maintained by women. This compares to 35 percent and 51 percent, respectively, in 1969.

7. It is frequently the wife's earnings that raise a family out of poverty. In husband–wife families in 1979, 14.8 percent were poor when the wife did not work; 3.8 percent when she was in the labor force. Of all wives who worked in 1979, the median contribution was more than one-fourth of the total family income. Among those who worked year round on a full-time basis, it was nearly two-fifths. Among black families, the median contribution of working wives was one-third of the total family income.[15]

During the last decade, various women's organizations worked to dispel the notion that women did not want better jobs, or that most of them preferred to stay at home. They worked toward asserting women's rights within the work force, gradually moved women into leadership positions and highlighted women's concerns during collective bargaining sessions, and supported women who ran for public offices. Women's caucuses insisted that public policies that reinforced domestic roles created self-images and behavior patterns that fostered inferior positions for women in the work force. In high schools and colleges all over the country, women's studies programs have been developed to satisfy demands for more and better information about women.

Some experts predict improvement for women as a result of shifts in the structure of work itself. Technological improvements have decreased the amount of physical strength needed to do most jobs, thus rendering groundless many physical reasons for discrimination against women. Even with these changes, it is painfully clear that much is left to be done in the war against discrimination. For example, Social Security benefits, still structured on the premise that each family has one breadwinner, have the net result of being more advantageous to women as dependents rather than as income earners. Furthermore, when women workers are unemployed, they face a dual discrimination. If they are pregnant, they may be denied unemployment benefits because they are not able to take another job. Also, women who give up jobs to follow their husbands who are relocated may not collect unemployment benefits in some states because they were not laid off.[16]

Pay and promotional opportunities are usually based on the official job description rather than actual performance. A disproportionate number of women are assistants who do much of their supervisor's work. In other instances, women workers may be performing the same duties as men for significantly different pay. Usually, the assistants are responsible for training the new executive; however, because the assistants belong to a certain sex, age, or racial group, they may find themselves discreetly blocked from joining the management staff, as well as locked into a dead-end job. This is true in many human service agencies.

As a result of discriminatory behavior, many women have the skills needed for upward mobility, but if these skills are not reflected on personnel records or job descriptions, a sex barrier is created, especially if there is a lack of initiative on the part of male administrators to give their female workers recognition when it is due. Interestingly, many women who achieve supervisory positions also discriminate against women. Ultimately, a large number of women discriminated against begin to discourage other women from thinking of themselves as having potential for higher-level jobs. These employees have become so convinced of their limited abilities that they lose the initiative to apply for training and promotion. They become a prophecy that fulfills itself. The effects of this not-too-subtle type of discrimination is evident in the higher ranks of many human service agencies' administrative staffs.

SEXUAL HARASSMENT. It is not uncommon for women to be subjected to unwelcome sexual advances, requests for sexual favors, and other verbal or physical conduct of a sexual nature. Although not illegal per se, such behavior is illegal when it is used by agency directors and supervisors to decide whether to hire or fire someone; when it is used to determine pay, promotion, or job assignment; and when it creates an intimidating, hostile, or offensive work environment. If an employee submits to sexual requests and receives job benefits from it, then the employer may be sued by the other employees who were equally qualified but denied similar benefits. "Examples of verbal harassment could include sexual comments, suggestions, jokes, or innuendos; nonverbal harassment could include suggestive looks, leering, or ogling; and physical harassment could include accidentally brushing against someone's body, 'friendly' pats, squeezes or pinches, and forced sexual relations."[17]

Sexual harassment is an outgrowth of individual and institutional sexist behaviors. Often it takes a considerable amount of courage for women to report harassment. Sexually harassed workers are embarrassed, intimidated, and demeaned. They become victims of external stress and frequently suffer from headaches, stomach pains, and inability to concentrate on job-related activities. Extreme stress leads to increased absenteeism, loss of efficiency, and reduced productivity. Employment turnover also increases because many harassed workers quit their jobs and rehiring and retraining costs go up.

RELIGIOUS INJUNCTIONS. The old masculinists believe that a woman is limited by her anatomy. Although the new masculinists support updating of women's roles, old masculinists—sometimes referred to as the backbone of the nation—prefer the status quo; that is, women should be preoccupied with finding husbands and raising children. Clearly, the ideas of the new feminist are counter to those of the old masculinist. The new feminist feels that sex roles have no place in the world of work, and the old masculinist feels that few women have any place in the world of work.

There are many biblical references to the roles of husband and wife: "Wives, submit yourselves unto your own husbands, as unto the Lord. For the husband is the head of the wife, even as Christ is the head of the church. . . . Therefore as the church is subject unto Christ, so let the wives be to their own husbands in every thing"

(Ephesians 5:22-24). "The aged women likewise, that they be in behaviour as becometh holiness, not false accusers, not given to much wine, teachers of good things; that they may teach the young women to be sober, to love their husbands, to love their children, to be discreet, chaste, keepers at home, good, obedient to their own husbands, that the word of God be not blasphemed" (Titus 2:3-5).

> The wives depicted in the historical writings exhibit a wide variety of characteristics, yet a coherent picture is not difficult to obtain. The good (ideal) wife is well-illustrated by Abigail, wife of Nabal (and later of David) (I Sam 25:2-42), with supplementary traits drawn from other examples. She is intelligent, beautiful, discreet, and loyal to her husband (despite his stupidity and boorish character in the case of Nabal; see Jer. 2:2). Prudent, quick-witted and resourceful, she is capable of independent action, but always acts in her husband's behalf. The good wife does not attempt to rule her husband, nor does she openly oppose him. She defers to him in speech and action, obeys his wish as his command, and puts his welfare first. She employs her sexual gifts for his pleasure alone and raises up children to his name.[18]

At best, the women's liberation movement is not an activity designed to force women to abandon their role as housewives but a concerted drive to provide equal opportunities in work situations outside the home for women who do not want to be primarily a wife or mother. A few overzealous feminists make the mistake of minimizing the importance and rights of those women who enjoy being wives and mothers.

Paul required that women refrain from fulfilling leadership roles in the church: "Let your women keep silence in the churches: for it is not permitted unto them to speak; but they are commanded to be under obedience, as also saith the law. And if they will learn any thing, let them ask their husbands at home: for it is a shame for women to speak in the church" (I Corinthians 14:34-35). Feminists have leveled sharp criticism at Paul for this and other views he expressed about women. Criticism is especially sharp for his view that woman was created expressly for man and that women should play a subservient role. In fairness to Paul, we should note that other passages attributed to him support women's equality. His insistence upon fidelity in marriage for both men and women renders a biblical injunction against double standards in sex morals. In fact, Paul's statement that "there is neither male nor female . . . in Christ Jesus" (Galatians 3:28) has been quoted frequently to support women's equality.

Generally, women who elect to leave their protective pedestals encounter problems in being accepted by men as equals. This is true even when women clearly illustrate their competence. Consequently, many women are criticized when their behavior parallels that of their male counterparts, and again when it does not. Even appearance can become an issue, as the flat-chested, bobbed-hair female styles of the 1920s and the pantsuits of the current times: "The woman shall not wear that which pertaineth unto a man, neither shall a man put on a woman's garment: for all that do so are abomination unto the Lord thy God" (Deuteronomy 22: 5).

An altering and meshing of sex roles will not occur easily. However, Caroline Bird is correct that "sex roles based on a division of labor between men and women are not inevitable just because they have been universal in the past."[19] Yet, because sex roles are tied to the Judeo-Christian ethic, change in this area is likely to be slow, and we should not be surprised if such change is accompanied by discord for several generations. In the end, the conservation and proper use of our human resources, female and male, will be the key in our efforts to save the earth's natural resources.

While there is no conclusive evidence to show that psychological and behavioral differences between the sexes are genetic or inherited, a great many differences do exist. It seems likely that culture provides the largest stimulus to certain types of behavior and attitudes among men and women. Regardless of the source, these differences do exist and present problems for females as employees in organizations.

Because of the predominant cultural role for women of homemakers and mothers, there is frequently a conflict between demands of the home and demands of the job. Mothers are more likely to display uneven work patterns because of childbirth and child rearing. They are more likely to request time off to care for a sick child. Some women actually prefer routine jobs that will not detract from their duties at home or compete with their husband's status and advancement. It is a difficult balancing act for human service employees who are torn between personal ambitions and family needs.

Special Programs

While it has been stated that the women's liberation movement is not the major reason for women's increasing participation in the work force, it is clear that the renewed interest in women's rights in the late 1960s had a significant impact on public policy. Antidiscrimination legislation can be credited in a large measure to pressure from feminists, many of whom worked in human service agencies. The problems of women may have originated at home, but public and private organizations have perpetuated sexism. These organizations now have the clear obligation to obey the laws enacted to end discrimination against women.

The Fourteenth Amendment to the United States Constitution provides that "no state shall deny to any person within its jurisdiction the equal protection of the laws." It would appear that this affords women constitutional protection of their rights; however, contrary to the Fourteenth Amendment, women have been treated so differently from men that the equal protection clause has not been meaningful to them. Three important federal laws and an Executive Order have been enacted to protect minorities and women.

THE EQUAL PAY ACT OF 1963 (EFFECTIVE JUNE, 1968). As an amendment to the Fair Labor Standards Act (FLSA), this act requires the same pay for men and women doing equal work, requiring equal skill, effort, and responsibility under similar working conditions in the same establishment. Where discrimination exists, pay rates of the lower-paid sex must be raised to equal those of the higher-paid sex. In a landmark decision, a federal court rejected a claim that the jobs of men and women have to be identical for them to receive equal pay and asserted that they need only be "substantially equal." The act, which is enforced by the Labor Department's Wage and Hour Division, permits wage differentials based on a bona fide seniority or merit system, or a system that measures earnings by quantity or quality of production, or any other factor other than sex.

TITLE VII OF THE CIVIL RIGHTS ACT OF 1964, AS AMENDED BY THE EQUAL EMPLOYMENT OPPORTUNITY ACT OF 1972: This legislation resulted in the creation of the Equal Employment Opportunity Commission (EEOC). Title VII prohibits discrimination in employment based upon sex, as well as on race, color, religion, and national origin, by employers of fifteen or more employees, public and private employment agencies, labor organizations with fifteen or more members and labor–management apprenticeship programs. Discrimination based on race, color, sex, religion, or national origin is unlawful in hiring and firing; wages; fringe benefits; classifying, referring, assigning, or promoting employees; extending or assigning use of facilities; training, retraining, or apprenticeships; or any other terms, conditions, or privileges of employment. The Equal Employment Opportunity Commission has issued guidelines that bar hiring based on stereotyped characterization of the sexes, classification or labeling of "men's jobs" and "women's jobs," or advertising under male or female headings. Also, the guidelines prohibit excluding from employment an applicant or employee because of pregnancy.

THE AGE DISCRIMINATION IN EMPLOYMENT ACT OF 1967 (EFFECTIVE JUNE, 1968): Administered by the secretary of labor, the law prohibits discrimination against people between the ages of forty and sixty-five in hiring, referral, classification, compensation, and other terms and conditions of employment (and related advertising) on the part of employers with twenty-five or more workers, employment agencies, and labor organizations.

EXECUTIVE ORDER 11246, AS AMENDED (EFFECTIVE 14 OCTOBER, 1968): This order prohibits employment discrimination based on sex, as well as on race, color, religion, or national origin, by federal contractors or subcontractors and contractors who perform work exceeding $10,000. To ensure nondiscrimination in employment, contractors must take affirmative action. Further, employers must state in all advertising that they are indeed affirmative/equal opportunity employers. According to revised orders, employers with over $50,000 in federal contracts and 50 or more workers must file affirmative action plans with goals and timetables with the Office of Federal Contract Compliance.

Laws and executive orders are not worth much if they are not monitored. Litigation pertaining to women's rights has accelerated over the past ten years, and women are winning a large share of them. For example, since 1977 more than 200 sexual harassment cases have been settled for over $10 million. Recent court actions against employers have resulted in women receiving back pay, promotions, reinstatement, attorney's fees, and unemployment compensation for sums ranging from $3000 to $200,000.

There are more qualified women and minorities for human service agency positions than any other career fields. Yet, women as a whole still tend to be found disproportionately in lower level clerical and professional positions. Equal employment opportunity programs that are the most effective do the following:

- Have a publicly shared affirmative action plan.
- Identify and abolish barriers to recruiting women.
- Encourage women to apply for all agency positions.
- Encourage and support women to take advantage of skill-training workshops, classes, and programs.
- Have a policy of promoting qualified women to supervisory positions.
- Publicly recognize supervisors who successfully recruit, train, and promote women.
- Have a procedure for dealing with personnel engaging in sexual harassment (e.g. verbal warning, written warning, probation, and termination). .
- Continually monitor their affirmative action progress.

Specific acts of discrimination may be difficult to pinpoint. However, statistics are essential tools that can be used to identify problem areas. Directors and supervisors have a significant impact on hiring, firing, training, promoting, delegating disciplinary action, and appraising and assigning agency employees. They control, directly or indirectly, the employment and advancement of women.

Techniques and Tips

One of the more significant conclusions of the many studies reviewed for this chapter is the need for procedures to aid and assist women workers in adjusting to their work environment. All employees have feelings, emotions, and attitudes that directly influence the quality of their work. The potpourri of behavior, hopes, fears, and emotions that human service workers bring with them to their jobs exerts tremendous influence on their professional growth. Therefore to be effective, women must adjust to some situations and challenge others, especially acts of discrimination.

One way to help employees adjust to their work environment is through individual counseling. Many agency supervisors believe that theories of counseling are fine, but in reality they are not very practical because of the lack of time. However, if done effectively career counseling can be an extremely valuable managerial tool for men with women workers. In fact, counseling is essential in establishing an open, honest climate with all subordinates, female or male. Even if they do not consider it counseling, supervisors must learn to listen to subordinates and help them to talk out their problems. The purpose of this is to promote a greater degree of understanding and possibly prevent acts of discrimination.

Directors and supervisors who dismiss the importance of counseling are extremely foolish. Like it or not, wherever a superior-subordinate relationship exists, counseling situations will inevitably arise. Therefore, to be an effective supervisor one must be an effective counselor. By its nature, employee counseling is broad. However, in some circumstances counseling may be for specific, predetermined reasons: (1) employment interviews, (2) job evaluations, (3) disciplinary cases, (4) morale surveys, and (5) exit interviews.

As stated earlier, workers bring their emotion with them to work. As a group, women are stressed by pressures of outside forces to a greater degree than their male counterparts. Not only must they adapt to the work environment, they must frequently adapt to changing family and sex roles. While this change impacts on both men and women, the values and attitudes of society put extraordinary pressure on women. Both male and female supervisors of women workers should consider the following dos and don'ts. First, supervisors in general and males in particular should:

1. *Have and be able to convey a genuine sensitivity for the concerns of women workers.* These concerns include (a) role

conflict and personal fragmentation that many women workers face as a result of being torn between the job and home, (b) lack of equity in pay, (c) inadequate promotion opportunities, (d) too few training opportunities, (e) occupational segregation, (f) sex discrimination, (g) sexual harassment, and (h) unfounded beliefs about what is appropriate behavior for men and women.

2. *Have an understanding of how interpersonal problems can affect an organization.* Supervisors must be aware of the woman worker as a person who frequently brings to work problems, values, and attitudes that affect her performance. It is important to remember that a woman's work performance may not reflect lack of commitment to the job.

3. *Get to know individual women workers and convey sensitivity to each worker in a noncondescending manner.* The supervisor must establish rapport with women workers and convey his or her desire to assist in problem solving and job enhancement.

4. *Be fair and insure that all staff members know and understand the agency's standards, policies, and procedures.*

5. *Listen carefully for negative and positive feelings.* Feed back this information, seek clarity, and understanding.

6. *Recognize the limits of their authority and expertise.* Know when it is appropriate to refer women workers to someone else or some other agency with more specialization in abating problems (e.g. marital, affirmative action, and chemical abuse specialists).

On the other hand, do not:

1. *Make unsubstantiated assumptions about women and what they can and cannot do.*
2. *Argue with or admonish women who need counseling.* This will cause them to become defensive and they will not share their feelings.
3. *Flaunt your authority (organizational or intellectual).* Talk *with* workers, not *at* them or *to* them.
4. *Give advice.* Help women by encouraging them to consider the advantages and disadvantages of various options to relieve job stress. Offer understanding of problems and answer questions about organizational policies and procedures. Ask questions, but allow workers to make the choice as to which option, if any, they will take.

Supervisors must learn, if they do not know already, how to deal effectively with women workers. Women are an extremely important human resource, absolutely essential to the functioning of human service agencies and the economic survival of our society. To unleash the full potential of this resource is an enormously complex task, but, on a smaller level, agency supervisors and co-workers can realize amazing gains by being sensitive to women's concerns and creating a climate where affirmative action is more than words.

EXERCISE DRILL

How to Deal With Sexual Harassment*

If a worker complains about sexual harassment, do your agency directors and supervisors:

- find out what action she (he) wants to take?
- offer to help by talking to the offending person privately or by meeting with the two of them together?
- advise the harassed worked to say "no" to the offender?
- follow the agency's disciplinary procedures if the offender repeats the harassment?

Under no circumstances should agency directors and supervisors:

- tell the harassed worker to ignore the harassment.
- assume that the worker "asked for it."
- joke about it.
- tell the worker to embarrass the harasser or to get physical.
- let the harassment continue.

If directors and supervisors see possible incidents of sexual harassment, but are not sure, do they:

- ask the potential victim if she (he) finds the behavior offensive or intimidating?
- tell the potential victim that she (he) does not have to accept harassment?

---

*Adapted from S.L. Webb: *Sexual Harassment: Guidelines for Supervisors and Managers* (Seattle: Pacific Resource Development Group, 1981, p.5).

The best remedy to harassment is *prevention*. Does your agency notify all employees with a written, posted policy statement that sexual harassment is illegal and will not be tolerated?

REFERENCES

1. Transou, C.G.: Emerging awareness in understanding sexism. *Delta Kappa Gamma Bulletin, 43*:50, 1977.
2. Mill, J.S.: The subjection of women. In Schneir, M. (Ed.): *Feminism: The Essential Historical Writings*. New York: Random House, 1972, p. 162.
3. Sigmund Freud. Quoted in Seldes, G. (Ed.): *Great Quotations*. New York: Pocket Books, 1967, p. 18.
4. Mill, J.S.: The subjection of women, p. 162.
5. Snow, K.M.: "My Liberated Mind has a Wuthering Heights Heart." *Harper's*, July 1973, p. 87.
6. Crigler, Pat: Quoted in Call, H.: "Why Does Activist Feminine Role Attract or Repel Some Women?" *San Diego Union*, October 21, 1973.
7. Ibid.
8. Ibid.
9. Syfers, Judy: Quoted in Klagsbrun, F. (Ed.): *The First Ms. Reader*. New York: Warner, 1973, pp. 23-25.
10. Riesman, David: Quoted in Bird, C.: *Born Female*. New York: Simon and Schuster, 1968, p. xiii.
11. Bowman, Gorda: Quoted in Bird, *Born Female*, p. 49.
12. Pifer, A.: "Women Working: Toward a New Society." Annual Statement of the President. New York: Carnegie Corporation, 1976, p. 1.
13. Farley, J.: *Affirmative Action and the Woman Worker*. New York: AMACOM, 1979, pp. 6-7.
14. United States Bureau of the Census: *A Statistical Portrait of Women in the U.S.* Washington, D.C., 1978, p. 41.
15. United States Department of Labor: *Twenty Facts on Women Workers*. Washington, D.C., 1980, pp. 1-3.
16. Kessler–Harris, A.: *Women Have Always Worked*. New York: McGraw–Hill, 1981, p. 155.
17. Webb, S.L.: *Sexual Harassment: Guidelines for Supervisors and Managers*. Seattle: Pacific Resource Development Group, 1981, p. 5.
18. Bird, P.: Images of women in the New Testament. In Ruether, R.R. (Ed.): *Religion and Sexism: Images of Women in Jewish and Christian Traditions*. New York: Simon and Schuster, 1974, p. 65.
19. Bird, C.: *Born Female*, p. 49.

Chapter 4
ETHNIC MINORITIES

MOST Americans can trace their ancestry back to some country across the oceans or the Mexican–American border. Each ethnic group has enriched our culture with its own particular types of music, food, customs, and dress. It usually takes two or more generations for the members of a new immigrant group to become sufficiently absorbed into the life of the community that they lose their separate identity. Some ethnic groups—mainly those of dark skin colors—never achieve total assimilation.

Those of us concerned about and committed to improving intergroup relations must guard against such clichés as "I'm not prejudiced" and "I treat all people the same." Even the most "liberal" helpers do not treat all people the same. As painful as it may be to admit, we are all prejudiced *for* or *against* other people. However, *it is behaviors, not attitudes, that comprise the major intergroup problems confronting us.* There are many laws against discriminatory behavior, but there are none against prejudicial attitudes.

The ethnic prejudices we find in our neighborhoods, schools, and jobs come from two main sources: first, the values and beliefs we learn from others and, second, the tensions and frustrations all of us experience while competing with other people, especially those who are culturally different. Race and racism continue to disrupt organization behaviors, even among well-educated professional helpers.

Definitions

Although outmoded geography books, using color as a criterion, once divided people neatly into five races—white, yellow, brown, black, and red—these arbitrary divisions have no validity, for there is no defensible means by which world populations can be precisely categorized: "Races, however defined, are not fixed entities with precise boundaries. Typologically defined races based on phenotypical likenesses do not correspond to genetic reality. In the light of modern genetics, races can best be defined as inter-breeding populations sharing a common gene pool."[1] In a consideration of racial matters, a much more practical dictum, and one too often unobserved, is that all living people belong to one and the same species and that the likenesses of our species are much greater than any differences that may be called "racial." Regardless of the manner chosen to define race, it has been found that the individual differences *within* races are greater than the differences *between* them, and that all individuals will vary to some degree in nearly every factor that combines to constitute human beings. Of far greater importance than the variations among humans are the similarities we have which inextricably involve each of us in all the implications of the human condition. Acknowledging this truth, many writers believe that incumbent upon us is the collective responsibility of creating a world in which other human beings are accorded the status of persons and not regarded as things or objects to be exploited.

The term *racism* derives from credence placed on the concept of race, for inherent in that concept is an acceptance of the validity of racial distinctions. Racism, in fact, implies that superior or inferior behavior is determined by race. In scholarly works, the term *scientific racism* is employed to describe a racial interpretation of history, or the belief that peoples of different races have different histories and cultures as a result of their race. However, the vast majority of anthropologists who study both race and culture contend that culture affects race much more than race affects culture. Despite this, in common parlance, the term racism connotes discrimination and prejudice. Commenting on this, Whitney Young defined racism as "the assumption of superiority and the arrogance that goes with it."[2] Almost 100 years earlier, Benjamin Disraeli had warned: "The difference of race is one of the reasons why I fear war may always exist; because race implies difference, difference implies superiority, and superiority leads to predominance."[3]

In any attempt to understand racism, distinctions need to be made among: (1) institutional structures and personal behavior and the relationship between the two; (2) the variation in both degree and form of expression of individual prejudice; and (3) the fact that racism is but one form of a larger and more inclusive pattern of ethnocentrism that may be based on any one of a number of factors, many of which are nonracial in character. A review of our culture clearly shows that the historical sources of American race relations are infinitely complex, and there is little doubt that racial bias and discrimination have been built into most American institutions. Ina Corrine Brown concluded, "The United States thus can be called a racist society in that it is racially divided and its whole organization is such as to promote racial distinctions."[4] In this frame of reference, the individual is necessarily a product of institutional racism, but expressions vary from person to person, both in degree and kind. It is also well to remember that what is commonly called racism is in part a segment of the larger problem of ethnic identification, of power and powerlessness, and of the exploitation of the weak by the strong.

To relegate human beings to less than full human status on the basis of their membership in a particular group, whether the group is based on race, class, or religion, is a phenomenon that has become increasingly intolerable to those who are oppressed. To abolish the dilemmas that stem from racism, institutional arrangements as well as personal behaviors must be drastically revised.

What we commonly call *race relations* should be properly understood in the larger context of *human relations*. Of particular concern should be the expression of attitudes and behavior by people toward others according to their identification as a member of a particular group. The expression of these attitudes and behavioral patterns is not innate but is learned as a part of the cultural process. Because of this, hope that they can be modified positively is justified. Negative group attitudes and destructive group conflicts are less likely to arise when helpers treat each other as individuals and respond to each other on the basis of individual characteristics and behavior. Students in introductory sociology classes learn that race-relations patterns are a part of our learned behavior or of our cultural patterns, and cultural patterns are but the sum and organization of a given people's way of thinking, feeling, and acting. These patterns are not unalterable, however, and with proper processes and patience lend themselves to modification: "Today with rapid communication and increased mobility, with the findings of science and the events of history generally made known, people everywhere are becoming aware of the alternatives to old ways. They have access to facts of history and interpretations of science that were previously unknown or unavailable to them. There have thus been opened up to them new conceptions of themselves and of other people. Much of the turmoil of the world today can be traced to the fact that modern communications and mobility have made people everywhere aware of cultural alternatives. All of these things are of the greatest significance in our changing patterns of race relations."[5]

In understanding racism, an important variable is the presence of *power*. It is the power to enforce the "prejudgment" of prejudice that leads to racism. Judy Katz wrote: "Racism is perpetuated by whites through their conscious and/or unconscious support of a culture and institutions that are founded on racist policies and practices. The racial prejudice of white people coupled with political, economic, and social power to enforce discriminatory practices on every level of life — cultural, institutional, and individual — is the gestalt of white racism."[6] Another important concept in understanding racism is the idea of *ownership of the problem*. Numerous writers define racism as a white problem, because white people developed it, perpetuate it, and have the power to end it. There is much credence in the proposition that the white American majority is in the best position to combat racism.[7]

Myths and Stereotypes

We are a nation founded on the religious teaching of Judaism and Christianity, which affirms the supreme worth of each human being. While they differ on many points of theology, Protestants,

Catholics, and Jews agree on the Brotherhood of Man under the Fatherhood of God. From this idea comes the basis for the common bond of all people. The words are right; the corresponding deeds are wrong. Few helpers live by the tenets of their religion. It is equally depressing to note that racist mobs are often made up of self-professedly religious people. An old slave prayer was dedicated to such people: "Lord, protect me from my friends, I know my enemies." Too many "religious" people believe that they are their brothers' keepers. People should free people, not keep them. The quest for freedom has caused several minority-group leaders to cry, "Free me or exterminate me!" Black Americans and Puerto Ricans have been kept too long in their slums and urban ghettos, Mexican Americans have been kept too long in migrant workers' camps, American Indians have been kept too long on reservations, and rural, poor whites have been kept too long on welfare.

Now, let us look at some erroneous beliefs pertaining to ethnic minorities in the United States.

1. *Every individual is not entitled to equal rights and dignity.* We cannot "grant" rights and dignity to others. They are entitled to them by the virtue of being human. This principle is embodied in the Golden Rule: "Do unto others as you would have others do unto you." Indeed, in the Judeo–Christian tradition we are to love our neighbors as ourselves. Little dignity accrues to people whom . we call niggers, dagos, honkies, freaks, greasers, wops, Christ killers, red savages, and so forth. Nor is it likely that recipients of such epithets will receive equal rights.

2. *The right to be free does not imply the right to be different.* The American Revolution was fought to free us from the tyranny of the British Empire, which limited our political thoughts and actions. A basic point of contention was the right to be different. Reminiscent of the English tyranny that led to the Revolution are the restrictive acts of the superpatriots who would silence individuals desiring to exercise *their* right to be different. In the 1960s, bumper stickers saying "America—Love It or Leave It" were countered by stickers saying "America—Change It or Lose It."

3. *Democracy can work for some without working for all.* "One nation under God, indivisible, with liberty and justice for

all" is but one way of saying that until all citizens are free, none are free. We form a human chain that is only as free or as enslaved as the individuals who make up its links. Despite Abraham Lincoln's warning that this country cannot continue to exist "half slave and half free," we seem determined to prove otherwise. Racial discrimination is pulling us apart as a nation, and economic discrimination is keeping us apart as groups.

4. *Minorities are happier with their own kind.* In the world of work, the few high-status minority employees take active part in the activities related to their jobs, while most low-status employees share in none at all. Acting as gatekeepers of job-related activities, high-status white workers resist broadening the base of participation to include low-status minority employees. "They need the time to improve their job skills" and "They wouldn't be happy with *our* crowd" are reasons frequently given for restricting the base of participation. Thus, minority employees are forced to form their own job-related organizations. Feeling left out and powerless, most minorities spend as little time as possible interacting with whites of equal or higher status.

5. *All we have to do to achieve equality is put people together.* Heterogeneous groupings have greater potential for behaving democratically than homogeneous groupings, but putting the bodies together does not ensure a democratic grouping. It takes considerable work and planning to make democracy a reality. "There's no need to waste our time working with those people," a white supervisor concluded; "Once a nigger always a nigger." He was talking about black workers, but he could just as well have been referring to Indians, Mexican Americans, Puerto Ricans, or other culturally different minorities. In a democratic society, it is imperative that formal and informal organizational activities do not become racially determined.

6. *Members of a particular minority group are all alike.* Individuals who do not know the various social class dimensions of ethnic minorities are also unlikely to know that despite common language, color, and historical backgrounds, all members of a particular minority group are not alike. It is presumptuous and counterproductive to talk about *the* black or *the* Indian or *the* Chinese as if members of these and other groups have only one set of

behavior characteristics. While this text will focus on ethnic group characteristics, the reader is reminded that social class differences often are more determinant of a minority worker's behavior than ethnic background.

Those Who Are Affected

Black Americans

Black children begin life facing higher survival odds than white children. They are more likely to die in infancy than white babies. If a black baby lives, the chances of losing his or her mother in childbirth is four times as high as the white baby. The black baby is usually born into a family that lives in the inner city (over 60% of the 25 million black-American population does). It is a family that is larger than its white counterpart, and it is crowded into dilapidated housing—quarters structurally unsound or unable to keep out cold, rain, snow, rats, or pests.[8]

With more mouths to feed, more babies to clothe, and more needs to satisfy, the black family is forced to exist on a median family income that is barely half the median white family income. When the black youngster goes to school, he or she usually finds it no avenue to adequate living, much less to fame or fortune. And because black children are generally taught in slum schools, with inferior teachers, equipment, and facilities, the education gap between black and white professionals of the same age often approaches two to three years.

In most communities heavily populated by black Americans, low-income and middle-income groups live in extremely close proximity to each other. This situation is not caused primarily by a "natural selection" process but rather by de facto housing segregation. Consequently, the plight of poverty-stricken black Americans is distorted if only census tract data are examined. Black "haves" appear less affluent and black "have nots" seem less disadvantaged than they actually are. There is, in short, a much wider gap between the black middle and lower classes than is statistically apparent. Both groups closely approximate their white counterparts in income and living styles. Low-income black Americans are a minority within a minority.

Black Americans are the most difficult ethnic group to categorize. The difficulty stems mainly from slavery, in which African heritages were almost entirely lost through assimilation with non-African cultures. Even so, the following generalizations typify traditional African-American cultural conditioning:

1. *Extended family.* The black family is sometimes extended bilaterally, but often it is maternally oriented. The black extended family is a closely knit group, frequently consisting of grandparents, aunts, uncles, nieces, nephews, and cousins. Within the black family, roles are interchanged more frequently than in most non-black families. This sharing of decisions and jobs in the home stabilizes the family during crisis situations.

2. *Kinship bonds.* Children born in and out of wedlock are loved. Legitimacy refers to parents; it has little to do with black children being accepted. Besides, children are proof of an individual's manhood or womanhood, and caring for them is proof of one's humanity. When children marry or otherwise reach adulthood, they leave home but often settle close to their parents or other relatives. Family unity, loyalty, and cooperation are part of the black life-style. (These values are also strongly held by the other ethnic groups discussed in this book.)

3. *Authority and discipline.* Childhood in the black community revolves around assertive behavior and challenging authority. There is a constant crossing of wills. Through this process, black children learn the acceptable limits of their behavior. Discipline tends to be harsh, strict, and preoccupied with teaching children respect for their elders, respect for authority, responsibility for themselves, and an understanding of what it means to be black in America.

4. *Religious orientation.* On the whole, black Americans are highly religious. Most of them are Protestant. The church offers spiritual hope to many persons who live in oppressive environments. The church also offers a facility for conducting nonreligious activities, such as Boy Scouts and Girl Scouts meetings.

5. *Achievement and work orientations.* Contrary to popular notion, most black parents pass on to their children high achievement aspirations. However, many black homes lack middle-class role models for children to emulate. The desire to achieve has

forced many black families to internalize a strong work orientation that makes palatable the unskilled and semiskilled jobs available in the discriminatory job markets within which most black Americans must work.

6. *Folk medicine.* African health practices make little distinction between physicians and nurses; both attend to the physical, emotional, and spiritual health of the patient. According to traditional African beliefs, both living and dead things influence an individual's health. In addition, health is directly related to nature. To be in harmony with nature is to have good health, whereas illness reflects being out of harmony with nature.

Mexican Americans

The eight million Mexican Americans reflect a variety of cultural patterns that are influenced by their parental heritage and the length of time their families have been American citizens. Second-generation and third-generation descendants of early Spanish settlers are usually affluent, but second-generation and third-generation descendants of agricultural workers tend to be poor. Still a third group is formed by the first-generation children of *braceros* —farm workers who have recently migrated from Mexico. The first two groups are likely to be Americanized; they have little knowledge of their Spanish heritage, and they speak little or no Spanish. Children of migrant workers speak fluent Spanish and hold tightly to Mexican customs and traditions. All Spanish groups are discriminated against by the Anglos—the white-American majority. In fact, in some communities Mexican Americans are the victims of more discrimination and segregation than black Americans.[9]

Census projections indicate that the total Hispanic-American population may soon exceed the black-American population. In addition to Mexicans and Puerto Ricans, a sizable number of legal and illegal immigrants come from Argentina, Peru, and Venezuela. Part of the difficulty in accurately counting and classifying Hispanic immigrants is due to the tendency of non-Puerto Rican Hispanics to list themselves as Puerto Rican to gain full rights as American citizens. In Texas and California, it is estimated that one million illegal immigrants entered from Mexico. The *barrios* (communities) tend to reflect the same economic and physical conditions as black neighborhoods.

In many ways, Mexican Americans epitomize both racial integration and cultural separatism. This duality is clearly seen in a brief review of Mexican history. The Aztecs were intermarried with their Spanish conquerors and with Indian tribes hostile to the Aztecs. The children of these mixed marriages were called *mestizos*. *Creoles,* pure-blooded Spanish people born in Mexico, largely disappeared through intermarriage. Blacks from Africa, brought into Mexico during the colonial period as slaves, married Indians, and their offsprings were called *zambos*. Zambos and mestizos later intermarried, causing the so-called Negro blood to disappear.

Although they are a racially mixed people, the heritage of Mexican Americans is quite similar. Some Mexican Americans prefer to be called *Chicanos*. The word "Chicano" stems from the Mexican-Indian Nahuatl word "Mechicano." The first syllable is dropped and "Chicano" is left. It is an old term for the American of Mexican descent. The Chicano movement (or Chicanismo) represents a commitment to the improvement of life for all Spanish-speaking Americans and Americans of Mexican descent.

Programs that work well for Mexican Americans may not work well for other Hispanic persons because of subcultural differences. For example, knowing that a person speaks Spanish may be inadequate cultural knowledge. There are qualitative differences in the language of Hispanics who are monolingual Spanish or bilingual Spanish–English. Furthermore, Spanish has many dialects—those brought to the United States by Hispanic immigrants and several that have developed in this country. A discussion of some of the common characteristics of Mexican Americans follows.

1. *La Raza (The Race)*. All Latin Americans are united by cultural and spiritual bonds believed to have emanated from God. Because God controls all events, Mexican Americans tend to be more present oriented than future oriented. The influence of the Roman Catholic church on *La Raza* is pervasive—Mexican Americans are born, get married, work, die, and are buried under the auspices of religious ceremonies.

2. *Family loyalty*. The familial role is the most important, and the family is the second most cherished institution in Mexican-American society. Chicanos owe their primary loyalty to the family. The worst sin is to violate one's obligations to the church and next comes the family.

3. *Respect*. The oldest man in the household is the family leader. Respect is accorded on the basis of age and sex. The old are accorded more respect than the young, and men are accorded more respect than women. Latino families are based on family solidarity and male superiority.

4. *Machismo*. Mexican culture prescribes that men are stronger, more reliable, and more intelligent than women. *Machismo* dictates that the man will show a high degree of individuality outside the family. Weakness in male behavior is looked down on.

5. *Compadrazgo*. The Mexican-American family is extended by the institution of *compadrazgo,* a special ceremonial bond between a child's parents and godparents. Often the bond between *compadres* is as strong as between brothers and sisters.

6. *Folk medicine*. Humoral pathology is an important aspect of Latin American and Spanish folk medicine. Their simplified form of Greek humoral pathology was elaborated in the Arab world, brought to Spain as scientific medicine during the period of Moslem domination, and transmitted to America at the time of the Spanish conquest. According to humoral medical beliefs, the basic functions of the body are regulated by four bodily fluids, or "humors," each of which is characterized by a combination of heat or cold with wetness or dryness.

Puerto Ricans

Puerto Rico is an island in the Caribbean approximately 1,000 miles from Miami and 1,600 miles from New York. Puerto Rico's population of over 3.5 million represents a density greater than that of China, India, or Japan. As a result of the Jones Act of 1917, all Puerto Ricans are American citizens. The island population is a mixture of Taino Indians, Africans, and Spaniards; Puerto Rican skin colors range from white to black, with shades and mixtures in between.[10]

Puerto Ricans who were raised on mainland America are sometimes called Neo-Ricans. The 1.7 million Neo-Ricans are mainly English speakers; few speak fluent Spanish. Despite dissimilar backgrounds, Puerto Ricans tend to be labeled black and subjected to the same prejudices inflicted on black Americans.

Many Puerto Ricans are reluctant to adopt American lifestyles. The following characteristics typify Puerto Rican culture:

1. *Sense of dignity.* Puerto Ricans demand that proper attention be given to culturally prescribed rituals, such as shaking hands and standing up to greet and say good-bye to people. A sense of dignity is present in all important interpersonal relationships.

2. *Personalismo.* Personal contact is established by Puerto Ricans before beginning a business relationship. It is important to exchange personal life data (such as size of family, their names, and their ages) before talking business.

3. *Individualism.* Puerto Ricans place high value on safeguarding against group pressure to violate an individual's integrity. This makes it difficult for Puerto Ricans to accept the concept of teamwork in which the individual relinquishes his or her individuality to conform to group norms. This characteristic reduces the importance of the Roman Catholic church in the lives of Puerto Ricans, most of whom are Catholic.

4. *Cleanliness.* Great emphasis is placed on being clean and well dressed. To some Puerto Ricans, looking good includes wearing bright colors and, frequently, styles rich in ornament.

5. *Fear of aggression.* Puerto Rican children are discouraged from fighting, even in self-defense. A Puerto Rican idiom describes this conditioning: *Juegos do mano Juego de villano* (pushing and shoving, even in play, makes one a villain). Survival in urban slum neighborhoods forces many Puerto Rican children to be villains.

6. *Compadrazgo and machismo. Compadrazgo* and *machismo* are operative in Puerto Rican culture in the same manner as in Mexican-American culture. Like blacks and Mexicans, Puerto Ricans love children, and illegitimacy is neither frowned on nor punished.

7. *Folk medicine.* For a discussion of Puerto Rican folk medicine, see the section pertaining to Mexican Americans. Both cultures are quite similar.

American Indians

There are approximately 400 Indian tribes and 900,000 Indians in the United States. Some are bilingual and others are not. Nor is there a common tribal language. This is why sign language became the major means of intertribal communication. Currently, American Indians and Alaskan natives are at the bottom of the economic ladder in the United States. They have the highest rates of unemployment and school dropouts, live in the most dilapidated housing, and in some parts of the country are accorded the lowest social status. These conditions reflect both what white Americans have done to the Indians and what the Indians have not been able to do for themselves.[11]

Unable to realize that we do not have an Indian problem but rather an American problem, the federal government has established government-controlled Indian bureaus, reservations, and assistance programs—including hospitals and clinics. Each of these short-sighted solutions has contributed to the psychological emasculation of Indian men, the demoralization of Indian women, and the alienation of Indian children. In other words, most government programs have failed to assist Indians in their efforts to maintain individual dignity and cultural identity while achieving success in the larger society.

Half the native-American population lives on 40 million acres of reservation in 30 states. Part of their plight is revealed in the following statistics. Indians have 100 million fewer acres of land today than in 1887. Their average life expectancy is 45 years. Nearly 60 percent of the adult Indian population has less than an eighth-grade education. Infant mortality is more than 10 percent above the national average. The majority of native-American families have annual incomes below $5000; 75 percent have annual incomes below $4000. Indian unemployment is almost ten times the national average.

Conflicts between white and Indian cultures are found on reservations, in small towns, and in big cities. The strain shows up in many ways, including juvenile delinquency, adult crime, and alcoholism. Historically, non-Indians have looked at Indian tribes but have failed to see the deplorable social, psychological, and physical deprivations. Some non-Indians tend to think that because an exceptional Indian has managed to succeed with little help, the others should also. Generally, the following characteristics apply to traditional American Indians:

1. *Present oriented.* Indians are taught to live in the present and not to be concerned about what tomorrow will bring. Non-Indians tend to be future oriented; they are constantly destroying the past and building the future.

2. *Time consciousness.* Many earlier Indian tribes had no word for time. Thus, historically the emphasis was placed on doing as opposed to going to do something or being punctual. Unlike non-Indians who rush to meetings to be punctual, Indians try to finish current activities. (Black Americans and Latinos have similar time consciousness.)

3. *Giving.* The Indian who gives the most to others is respected. In many tribes, saving money or accumulating consumer goods results in ostracism.

4. *Respect for age.* Like the other ethnic groups discussed in this book, respect for the Indian increases with age. Indian leadership is seldom given to the young.

5. *Cooperation.* Indians place great value on working together and sharing resources. Failure to achieve a personal goal is believed to be the result of competition.

6. *Harmony with nature.* Indians believe in living in harmony with nature. They accept the world as it is and do not try to destroy it. Along with this belief goes a belief in taking from the environment only what is needed to live.

7. *Extended family.* The American Indian family network is radically different from other extended family units in the United States. The typical non-Indian extended family includes three generations within a single household. American Indian families include several households representing relatives along both vertical and horizontal lines. Grandparents are official and symbolic family leaders. In addition, namesakes (formalized through a religious ceremony) become the same as parents in the family network.

8. *Folk medicine.* The Indian medicine man is a vivid reminder that long before physicians, nurses, social workers, and counselors intruded into their lives, native Americans had folk cures for physical and mental illnesses. Upon reflection, it is no more logical to believe in germs that we cannot see than in spirits whom we cannot see. An example of Indian folk medicine is seen in traditional Navajo culture that asserts that illness is a sign that a person is out of harmony with nature. Indian religion and medicine are virtually indistinguishable. Medicine men, singing, rituals, and chants are important aspects of treatment for illness.

Asian Americans

The plight of poverty-stricken Asian Americans is vividly captured in Los Angeles and San Francisco Chinatown statistics: more than one-third of the Chinatown families are poverty stricken; three-fourths of all housing units are substandard; rents have tripled in the past five years; more than half the adults have only a grade school education; juvenile delinquency is increasing; and the suicide rate is three times the national average. Most of the two million Asian Americans, however, are neither poverty stricken nor poorly educated.[12] Many of the following values that characterize traditional Chinese are applicable to most traditional Asian cultures:

1. *Filial piety.* There is unquestioning respect for and deference to authority. Above all else, there is the expectation that each individual will comply with familial and social authority.

2. *Parent—child relationship.* Children defer to their parents, especially in communication, which is one-way from parents to children.

3. *Self-control.* Strong negative feelings are seldom verbalized. Assertive and individualistic people are considered crude and poorly socialized.

4. *Fatalism.* Resignation and pragmatism characterize the manner in which Chinese Americans deal with change in nature and social settings.

5. *Social milieu.* Chinese Americans are other-directed and therefore greatly concerned with how their significant others view and react to them. Social solidarity is highly valued.

6. *Inconspicuousness.* Taught to avoid calling attention to themselves, Chinese Americans are likely to be silent in public settings.

7. *Shame and guilt.* Since Chinese Americans are taught to respect authority and maintain filial piety toward their parents and their ancestors, a violation of this cultural norm results in feelings of shame and guilt. The Chinese family is a continuum from past to future whose membership includes not only the present generation but also the dead and the unborn.

8. *Folk medicine.* Asian folk medicine and philosophies have a strong Chinese influence. Unlike Western medicine, which empha-

sizes disease and cure, Asian medicine focuses on prevention. The theoretical and philosophical foundation of Chinese medicine is the Taoist religion, which seeks a balance in all things. Both energy (*Chi*) and sexual energy (*Jing*) are vital life energies, with Chi and Jing kept in balance by *Yin* and *Yang*. Yin is feminine, negative, dark, and cold; whereas Yang is masculine, positive, light, and warm. According to Chinese medicine, an imbalance in energy is caused by an improper diet or a strong emotional feeling. Balance or good health may be achieved through the use of appropriate herbs.

Whether or not to integrate into Western society is a question that most ethnic minority professionals ponder. This is an especially sensitive issue for individuals subscribing to traditional cultural values. The dilemma is somewhat similar to that of the early European immigrants to the United States. When they initially came to this country during the nineteenth century, the Poles, Greeks, Germans, Italians, and other groups clustered together in their own ethnic enclaves. Gradually, either they or their children moved out of their ethnic neighborhoods into the larger community. Along with this change came a merging of languages, customs, habits, dietary patterns, and housing.

While the European ethnic groups were assimilating into a nebulous American melting pot, the other people present at that time were not. Some minority group activists argue that *pluralism*, not assimilation, is the most viable goal for all people. Switzerland and Canada are examples of pluralism that may be the most acceptable to this group:

> The standard example of cultural pluralism is Switzerland, a country that maintains a high degree of national unity although it has no national language and is religiously divided. In Switzerland, Protestants and Catholics have been able to live agreeably under the same government, while speaking either German, French, or Italian. Since the Swiss citizen does not feel that either his religious loyalty or his ethnic identification is threatened by other Swiss, he is free to give complete allegiance to the Swiss nation as a common government that allows for the tolerance of distinctly different cultural groups. Canada, with a division between the French and the English, and Belgium, with a division between the French and the Flemish-speaking populace, are other examples of cultural pluralism. The different groups

that make a pluralistic society in these nations frequently engage in a struggle for influence, but the essential ideal is that national patriotism does not require cultural uniformity and that differences of nationality, language, or even race do not preclude loyalty to a common government.[13]

Within a similar framework, it would be possible for ethnic minorities to move into desegregated jobs and neighborhoods without losing other aspects of their ethnicity.

Special Programs

Equality of treatment and opportunity has been the official policy of some organizations for many years. In their standards of recruitment, training, and group relations, government and public human service agencies have been more effective as equal-opportunity employers than the private business sector. But even in government and human service agencies there is room for improvement. Most equal-opportunity employers are merely paper compliers; their behavior is anything but exemplary of equality in action.

The policy of equal employment opportunity (EEO) is applied without regard to sex, race, creed, color, or national origin. An important first step toward equality of opportunity is the recognition that many influential members of organizations do harbor prejudices and that they do not put these prejudices aside when they are on the job. Unless administrators carefully monitor on-the-job activities, prejudices will be manifested in official and semiofficial actions.

Administrators must not assume that it is adequate merely to issue memoranda and directives setting forth the policy of equal opportunity. They must find out for themselves whether their subordinates are accorded equal treatment. The following are several effective methods by which an administrator can make certain that his or her organization understands the policy of equal opportunity:

1. Discuss the policy in staff conferences.
2. Discuss the policy in informal talks with subordinates.
3. Issue periodic statements of the policy in newsletters or memoranda.
4. Explain the policy during the orientation of new employees.

Resolving cases involving discrimination always involves value judgments. Administrators should, however, try to abate discriminatory practices in such a way as to cause those doing the discriminating to alter their behavior. Transferring the individual being discriminated against or transferring the discriminator does not solve the problem; it merely leaves the discriminator free to repeat the act. *Good human relations cannot be delegated — they begin and end with each of us.*

Essential to any affirmative action problem-solving effort is a provision for *feedback*, a sharing of honest feelings. Problem-oriented feedback allows feelings to be expressed as directly and as clearly as possible. Often it is accomplished by such simple statements as "I am angry" or "I feel hostile." Ideally, these feelings are related as much as possible to the factors believed to have caused them. Thus, more definitive feedback would be "I am angry because I was not promoted, and I believe I am better qualified than the people who were promoted." This technique is based on the assumption that feelings *do* exist and should not be considered irrelevant or disruptive of a smoothly functioning organization. Those who would dismiss feelings as irrelevant would deny the humanity of humans.

Most minorities prefer to express their real feelings, but when they believe that nothing will be done to solve their problems or that they will be penalized for expressing their views, they are likely to conceal their real feelings. Only when they are convinced that their opinions are to be given a fair hearing will most people be honest in expressing them.

Issues centering on race or color often cause administrators and their subordinates to overreact. In such instances it is difficult to sort out fact from fiction, and objectivity from subjectivity, but it must be done. The development of excessive ego defenses by members of a minority group is especially disturbing to those who are unaware that they have done something to elicit such behavior. Most administrators want their subordinates to like them, but their behavior is anything but conciliatory. As an angry black female employee observed, "They don't even know my name or that I exist." A smile or a nod — a friendly acceptance of the person — may prevent a labor–management dispute.

A member of an organization who understand the other members, wins their confidence, and perceives alternatives for meeting their needs is able to help them become effective members of the group. This kind of leader does not run from people; instead, he or she runs to them and is received with enthusiasm. Group members who are preoccupied with sorting out colors, races, and social classes are not likely to treat all members fairly. They cannot communicate to rejected members that they care, because they do not. Members of organizations who care about others behave as though they are color blind, realizing that they are interacting with *people,* not colors.

Most minorities join organizations wanting to be accepted. To be cared about by the various members of the organization is a sign of social worth. To be cared about by individual members whom they like and respect is to become someone very special. People who feel a need to move *away* from others are frightened, and those who move *against* members of the organization are angry. Neither the frightened nor the angry feel secure with leaders who indicate that they do not care about them.

The laws and regulations cited in Chapter 3 apply to minorities too. It cannot be said too often that good human relations center on treating every individual as an individual, respecting his or her "selfhood," and being willing to change if our behavior is wrong. The first step in resolving intergroup conflict is to understand the other persons' point of view. To do so, we must allow them the freedom to participate in decisions that affect their welfare. Most human relations problems proceed from lack of information, lack of human relations skills, and decisions that are inadequate to resolve the given problem. Most human relations problems can be resolved by:

1. Following equal opportunity regulations and exercising proper jurisdiction.
2. Getting all the facts.
3. Correctly analyzing the facts.
4. Involving all persons in the deliberations.
5. Assigning responsibility for corrective action.
6. Following up to see that corrective action is carried out.

The process of getting the facts involves both verbal and non-verbal comunication. *How* something is said is just as important as *what* is said. *What is not said* is also important. (See Exercise 1) Good human relations involves learning to listen. Many organizational problems have been quickly and effectively solved by individuals who decided to listen before rendering a decision.

Techniques and Tips

Ethnic minority workers tend to take their cues from nonminorities. Insensitivity to a worker's beliefs and fears may result in premature termination of a personal consultation. Most minority workers need time to talk, to listen, and to learn about job opportunities and equal opportunity practices. Relatedly, supervisors who tell minority workers not to be embarrassed or feel guilty because they do not fully understand agency procedures may inadvertently suggest that they *should* experience those feelings.

When minority needs are expressed and received, the distance between minority and majority group workers is spanned. As the minority–majority relationship unfolds, the special background of the supervisor comes to the center of the interaction. Both verbally and nonverbally, an effective supervisor will communicate expertise. For most minority-group workers this means becoming exposed to new ways of defining and treating their employment needs. New ways are not always easy to accept.

It is important for the supervisor to explain the technical aspects of job opportunities or complaint procedures in terms that will make sense to all workers. If minorities are to willingly and accurately pursue opportunities, they must understand and accept their supervisor's suggestions. This is a basic human relations principle: *individuals affected by an affirmative action plan must understand it if optimum satisfaction is to occur.*

When the minority worker is nourished and sustained by contact with a non-minority administrator, the relationship is not only good but also helpful. We all would do well to remember that most people are like the Philosopher in James Stephen's *The Crock of Gold*, who said, "I have learned that the head does not hear anything until the heart has listened, and that what the heart knows today the head will understand tomorrow."[14]

Administrators have feelings, too, and part of their professional skill is the management of them. Administrators have feelings of likes and dislikes, happiness and grief, security and insecurity, competence and incompetence. They may be strongly attracted to some workers and repelled by others. In short, they respond to minorities with feeling. The challenge is to minimize unfair, nonprofessional treatment and to maximize fair, professional treatment of *all* workers.

The problems of intergroup communication are more complex than many authors suggest. Seldom is a professional helper taught to elicit transcultural information (i.e. how to talk, listen, and provide feedback, but this is not to suggest that there are no white professionals who can effectively communicate with ethnic minority people. There are many who possess this skill, though most of them are self-taught. Something as important as transcultural communication should not be left to intuition or chance; nor should the minority worker's understanding of the nonminority worker.

Numerous studies conclude that a large number of minority workers receive insufficient information about their present job conditions and future opportunities. Specifically, many minorities leave agencies without ever having understood what their supervisors diagnosed as their needs, why certain procedures were followed, and, if failure resulted, what their failures consisted of and the reasons for them. The minority worker's rights include the right to courteous, prompt, and the best treatment and the right to know what is wrong, why, and what can be done about skill deficiencies.

We could build a case of minority worker ignorance as being a by-product of the helping profession's mystique. That is, helping professions are commonly perceived as being administered by white men whose training and predilections place them in a special ability category. To put it even more bluntly, there is a tendency for ethnic minority workers to be in awe of white, male administrators, but beyond this intagible dimension of the communication process, supervisors remain divided over what information should be given to minorities and how that information should be given.

It is likely that minority workers who are the most confused about their condition and what their supervisors are doing or did for them are less actively involved in discussions about their careers than minorities who are better informed. Unfortunately, most supervisors cannot accurately judge the level of their subordinates' knowledge. An old adage seems appropriate: when in doubt, ask. There are several ways the more effective supervisors communicate with ethnic minority workers. Some supervisors verbally tell their subordinates the information; others use printed materials, including diagrams and leaflets. Still others refer workers to commercial audiovisual material. A few use all of these methods. In the end, the quality of the information a supervisor is able to give a worker is directly related to the quality of information he or she gets from the worker. Additional tips are:

1. Call minorities by their right names. In Spanish, for example, people are given two last names. The first last name is from the father's family and the second last name is from the mother's family. Use both last names so as not to insult the client. Also, ask the worker for the correct pronunciation of his or her name and use it.
2. Try to understand local minority customs.
3. Study local minority histories.
4. Analyze your feelings about various ethnic minority groups.
5. Avoid patronizing or condescending approaches to minority clients and workers.
6. When giving information, don't merely ask individuals if they understand what you have said; ask them to repeat it.

ETHNIC DIFFERENCES. The challenge to the administrator is to demonstrate that competence and empathy are not unique to members of a particular group. For example, a competent white administrator can be as "black" as any of the black employees in his or her organization. Blackness is more than a condition of the skin; it is thinking black, behaving black, and accepting black. Just as blacks grudgingly admit that some white people have "soul," whites will acknowledge that some black people have "culture." Skin color may be a help or a hindrance in establishing rapport.

Individuals who are most different from minority-group workers in terms of culture generally have more difficulty communicating empathy, congruence, respect, and acceptance than individuals who share or understand the workers' cultural perspectives. To be more specific, non-white workers who understand the psychological and sociological backgrounds of non-white workers are better able to counsel minorities than their colleagues who lack this knowledge. Yet, a meaningful relationship with a white worker representing the dominant society can do much to reduce hostile minority-worker feelings. Indeed, the helping process is a rare opportunity for understanding ethnic group differences and similarities.

In the end, the most successful human relators are (1) linguistically compatible with ethnic minority workers, (2) empathic, and (3) well trained. This means that the initial edge a helper will have who is from the same ethnic group as the worker will be lost if the helper cannot go beyond ethnic history and identity. When accepting a position, minority workers want professionally and culturally competent supervisors and colleagues.

REFERENCES

1. Brown, I.C.: *Understanding Race Relations.* Englewood Cliffs, NJ: Prentice–Hall, 1973, p. 44.
2. Young, W.M., Jr.: *Beyond Racism: Building an Open Society.* New York: McGraw–Hill, 1969, p. 73.
3. Disraeli, B.: *British House of Commons,* February 1, 1849.
4. Brown, *Race Relations,* p. 8.
5. Ibid., p. 22.
6. Katz, J.H.: *White Awareness: Handbook for Anti-Racism Training.* Norman: University of Oklahoma Press, 1978, p. 10.
7. Atkinson, D., Morten, G., and Wing, D.: *Counseling Minorities: A Cross-Cultural Perspective.* Dubuque, IA: William C. Brown, 1979, p. 205.
8. Henderson, G. (Ed.): *Understanding and Counseling Ethnic Minorities.* Springfield: Thomas, 1979, pp. 29–30.
9. Samora, J. (Ed.): *La Raza: Forgotten Americans.* South Bend: University of Notre Dame Press, 1966.
10. Maldonado-Denis, M.: *Puerto Rico: A Socio-Historic Interpretation.* New York: Vintage Books, 1972.
11. Deloria, V., Jr.: *God is Red.* New York: Grosset & Dunlap, 1973.
12. Sue, S., and Sue, D.W.: Understanding Asian-Americans: The neglected minority. *Personnel and Guidance Journal, 5:*387-389, 1973.

13. Horton, P.B.: *Sociology and the Health Sciences.* New York: McGraw-Hill, 1965, pp. 310–311.
14. Stephens, J.: *The Crock of Gold.* New York: Macmillan, 1945, p. 128.

Chapter 5
ALCOHOLICS

ALCOHOLISM is a major health problem among social agency personnel. To date, researchers have been unable to find any simple remedies for this problem. The human and financial waste is frightening. If we are to prevent the abuse of alcohol, we first must understand the people who become alcoholics, their reasons for drinking, and the ways in which it affects them. Similarly, we need to understand the factors that encourage other human service personnel to drink responsibly.

Most workers who drink alcoholic beverages do so to obtain feelings of pleasure, as well as to gain relief from the stress of their jobs. Others drink to have fun or because their peers are drinking. Some take only an infrequent drink, while others drink continuously. Some drink to achieve a special feeling of identity, a rapport with their fellow workers; some drink to escape from themselves and others. Some can take it or leave it; some can neither take it nor leave it. Some drink only wine, some drink only beer, some drink only distilled spirits, and some drink anything they can find. Some drink during religious rituals; others do not drink because of religious beliefs.

A few workers drink because they believe that alcohol taken in small amounts has special medicinal value; others abstain because they believe that even in small amounts, alcohol is injurious to their health. Some workers drink because of what they believe alcohol does for them; others refrain because they dislike what they fear alcohol does to them. In some homes alcohol is strictly forbidden; in others it is found on the table at every meal. Some workers are inflexible in their belief that alcoholic beverages are for adults only; others give their children wine or beer at mealtime.

Definitions

Throughout history, what we now call alcoholism has been considered a problem, and moderation has been the most frequently recommended, commonsense remedy. One of the oldest temperance writings was done in Egypt about 3000 years ago, under the title of "Wisdom of Ani": "Take not upon thyself to drink a jug of beer. Thou speakest, and an unintelligible utterance issueth from thy mouth. If thou fallest down and thou break limbs, there is none to hold out a hand to thee. Thy companions in drink stand up and say, 'Away with this sot.' And thou act like a little child."[1] Today, there are many sots working in social agencies.

There are hundreds of definitions of alcoholism, including the one adopted by the World Health Organization: "Any form of drinking which in its extent goes beyond the traditional and customary 'dietary' use or the ordinary compliance with the social drinking customs of the whole community concerned, irrespective also of the extent to which such etiological factors are dependent upon heredity, constitution or acquired physiopathological and metabolic influences."[2] An alcoholic has been defined as "one who repeatedly seeks to change reality through the use of alcohol"[3] and "one who suffers because of uncontrolled compulsive drinking."[4] For our purposes, the following definition may serve as a useful guide in evaluating a drinker: "An alcoholic is one whose drinking interferes with his health, his job, his relations with his family, or his community relationships and yet he continues to drink."[5] The fact that the alcoholic continues to drink implies a loss of control, which is the primary characteristic of an illness. The interference need only be felt in one of the vital areas for a person's classification as an alcoholic.

These definitions apply to all social and economic classes. Less than 6 percent of the alcoholics in the United States are found on skid row. The other 95 percent to 97 percent can be found in places where "solid citizens" congregate. The definitions apply to men, women, and children alike. Although it was once thought that male alcoholics outnumbered female alcoholics by about 5 to 1, it is now agreed that the ratio is approaching 1 to 1.

Despite the fact that alcoholism is labeled a disease by the American College of Physicians, the American Medical Association, the American Psychiatric Association, the World Health Organization, and other scientific bodies, a large segment of our population still views it as a moral weakness. This latter view creates problems for many alcoholics receiving treatment.

This disease is 100 percent fatal; nobody survives unchecked alcoholism. Death is usually slow and painful. It is estimated that 10 percent of the drinkers in America will become alcoholic and will not be able to stop drinking by themselves. Four significant characteristics of the disease are that it is primary, progressive, chronic, and fatal.[6] Although this paints a grim picture for the drinking alcoholic, there is hope for the individual suffering from this disease. With help, the psychological and physical progression of alcoholism can be stopped and the alcoholic can be recovered. This necessarily involves the whole person, which includes the physical, mental, psychological, and spiritual aspects of the individual. A treatment plan is not likely to be successful if it does not provide treatment for all four areas simultaneously.

The term *chemical dependency* is used to include drug dependencies and drug addictions as well as alcoholism. It is important to note that ethyl alcohol is a drug, even if society does not always view it as such.

THE COST. There are 100 million Americans over the age of 15 who are classified as drinkers. Of this number, an estimated 9 million are alcoholics. Ninety-five percent of the alcoholics are found in middle-class America. A conservative estimate is that 4 million of America's alcoholics are women. Four to eight percent of our work force suffer from this disease. Fifty percent of all fatal automobile accidents involve alcohol. Forty percent of all male admissions to state mental hospitals suffer from alcoholism. Thirty-one percent of those who take their own lives are alcoholics. Forty percent of the problems brought to family courts are the result, directly or indirectly, of alcoholism. For each problem drinker, an average of four other persons are directly affected.[7]

In 50 percent of all homicides, the victim or the one who committed the crime, or both, had been drinking. Forty-nine percent of all suicide victims were drinking at the time of their death.

According to a New Mexico study, 50 percent of rapes have an incidence of alcohol.[8]

All citizens absorb the costs created by the many physical and psychological repercussions of alcoholism. Over $50 million is spent each year for the care of alcoholics in state institutions. This figure does not include the cost to insurance companies. Some mental hospitals estimate that 80 percent to 90 percent of their first admissions are alcoholics. A conservative estimated loss sustained by industry because of alcoholic employees is $10.4 billion.[9] Ruth Fox succinctly defined the overall situation in 1959. The only change is in the lives and money wasted, and these have increased significantly.

> If some new and terrible disease were suddenly to strike us here in America—a disease of unknown cause possibly due to a noxious gas or poison in our soil, air, or water—it would be treated as a national emergency with our whole citizenry uniting as a man to fight it. Let us suppose the disease to have so harmful an effect on the nervous system that five million persons in our country would go insane for periods lasting from a few hours to weeks or months and recurring repeatedly over periods ranging from fifteen to thirty years. Let us further suppose that during these spells of insanity, acts of so destructive a nature would be committed that the material and spiritual lives of whole families would be in jeopardy, with a resultant twenty-five million persons cruelly affected. Work in business, industry, professions and factories would be crippled, sabotaged or left undone. And each year more than 1.25 billion dollars would need to be spent merely to patch up in some small way the effects of the disease on families whose breadwinner had been stricken. Finally, let us imagine this poison or disease to have the peculiar property of so altering a person's judgment, so brainwashing him that he would be unable to see that he had become ill at all; actually so perverting and so distorting his view of life that he would wish with all his might to go on being ill. Such an emergency would unquestionably be classed as a country-wide disaster, and billions of dollars and thousands of scientists would be put to work to find the cause of the disease, to treat its victims and to prevent its spread. The dread disease envisioned above is actually here. It is ALCOHOLISM.[10]

Myths and Stereotypes

Alcohol problems and their management are best understood within the context of public and private beliefs about the use and abuse of alcohol. Despite considerable mass media information about the effects of alcohol, there remains mass ignorance. Within the next few pages we will examine some of the more common myths and stereotypes as well as factual information about alcohol and alcoholism.

1. *"You are not an alcoholic unless you drink a pint of liquor a day."* There is no simple rule of measurement as to who is an alcoholic. However, experts have concluded that how much we drink is far less important than when we drink, how we drink, and where we drink. Because we learn to adapt our drinking behavior so that we can consume more alcohol and show less effect, it is harder to notice and easier to deny that we are becoming intoxicated.

2. *"Alcoholism is just a state of mind."* On the contrary, it is also a physiological illness. After long-term, heavy use of alcohol, our tolerance begins to be reduced. This happens because alcohol damages body organs, such as the brain and the liver. A damaged liver reduces the body's ability to eliminate alcohol, while a damaged brain distorts and impairs our decision making.

3. *"Most alcoholics are skid row bums."* Most alcoholics are *not* skid row bums. Approximately 70 percent of American alcoholics are "solid citizens."

4. *"A few minutes of sweating in a hot shower will sober a person up."* Most (95%) alcohol leaves the bloodstream through a process called *metabolic oxidation*: it is broken down into carbon dioxide and water by the liver. The rest (5%) of the consumed alcohol leaves the body through breath, urine, and perspiration. At most, up to 10 percent of consumed alcohol may be eliminated through breath, urine, and sweat if a high blood alcohol level is maintained. Thus, it is almost impossible to sweat enough to sober up.

5. *"I just had a big meal, I can't get drunk."* A full stomach does retard the passage of alcohol into the small intestine. Food and drink also dilute the concentration of alcohol in the small intestine and, therefore, reduce the rate of alcohol absorption into the blood. However, if a sufficient amount of alcohol is consumed, a person will become intoxicated on a full stomach.

6. *"All I have to do to sober up in a hurry is drink plenty of black coffee and walk in the fresh air."* Black coffee or other hot beverages, fresh air, and long walks may pass time but they will not change the rate at which alcohol is oxidized by the liver. Besides, stimulants such as coffee only counteract alcohol's depressant action and turn a sleepy drunk into a wide-awake one.

7. *"Social drinkers don't have drinking problems."* A large number of "social drinkers" become alcoholics. It matters little whether we drink alone or with other persons, we may become an alcoholic if we become chronic drinkers.

8. *"I need a few drinks before an important meeting to get control of myself."* While it is true that alcohol tends to reduce our inhibitions and shyness, it is not true that it gives us more or greater self-control. Alcohol releases a wide range of feeling (e.g. anger, hostility, overconfidence, jealousy, and generosity, to mention a few). All of these feelings may result in unusual or inappropriate behavior for the drinker (e.g. crying, fighting, laughing, nagging, and risk taking).

9. *"I'm a better driver when I have a few drinks; my reflexes are sharper."* Three or four drinks have the potential of reducing our ability to judge distances, speed, and angles; reducing our ability to judge our own abilities; causing forgetfulness; and causing sleepiness. It is a truism that drinking and driving do not mix.

10. *"I don't know any alcoholics."* Some of your most respected colleagues and best friends may be alcoholics and you are unaware of it. Most alcoholics are adroit at hiding their drinking problem from other persons and themselves.

Alcohol affects different people differently, and often it affects the same people differently at different times. There is no clear-cut evidence that moderate drinking has any lasting harmful effects on the body or mind. However, there is strong evidence that excessive drinking has permanent harmful effects on the body. Alcohol helps most drinkers to relax, forget minor worries, relate to people better, and have more fun. Too much alcohol does none of these things.

Those Who Are Affected

Who contracts this illness? What kinds of people become alcoholic? As noted earlier, the answer seems to be that all kinds of people can become alcoholic. No one knows why some drinkers continue to drink and never experience the symptoms of alcoholism, while others continuously experience difficulty and become alcoholic. Many experts believe that it is a combination of physical, psychological, and sociological causes. There exists enough empirical evidence to suggest that alcoholics show a cluster of personality traits once their drinking patterns have been established. Included in the cluster are low stress tolerance, dependency, perceptual dependence, negative self-image, and feelings of isolation, insecurity, and depression. However, the problem of interpretation centers on whether such traits precede the alcoholic behavior or whether the cluster of traits is a consequence of the addiction.[11]

There are different types of alcoholics and different kinds of alcoholism, so it is dangerous to generalize, but an alcoholic is usually the last to accept his or her illness. Denial of a drinking problem appears to be an inherent trait of alcoholics. For example, if an alcoholic is asked his definition of an alcoholic, he will give a definition that does not include himself. If he never drinks before noon, then his definition of an alcoholic is an individual who drinks before noon. If he drinks only at home, his definition of an alcoholic will be one who drinks at bars. If he drinks at bars, then an alcoholic is one who drinks at home.

Professional helpers are exposed to certain working conditions that contribute to the development of alcohol problems and other stress-related problems, including the following:

1. *Absence of clear agency goals*: lack of clearly stated criteria to evaluate work and little or no feedback to worker about performance.
2. *Freedom to determine work hours*: the worker can cover up what would otherwise be absenteeism.
3. *Low structural visibility*: the job requires time away from other workers, leading to estrangement from fellow workers and from people important to one's personal life.
4. *Work addiction*: literally living, breathing, and eating work.
5. *Occupational obsolescence*: the meaning or value of one's work is no longer important.
6. *New work statuses*: new roles are acquired that are ambiguous.
7. *Required on-the-job drinking*: drinking to entertain clients or individuals who may support the agency.

8. *Mutual benefits*: when it pays one worker to get another drunk
so that he or she may advance at the other's expense.
9. *Severe role stress*: when the job creates great pressure.[12]

There are some distinct behavioral and emotional phases of
alcoholism. In reviewing these phases, it is easier to understand
why alcoholics are unable to see what is happening to them. As
their disease gets progressively worse, their self-image continues to
deteriorate and their ego strength ebbs. They are unable to keep
track of their own behavior and begin to lose contact with their
loved ones. The greater the pain, the higher and more rigid the defenses become. The result is that alcoholics become victims of
their own defense mechanisms.

In 1946, after making an extensive analysis of available data,
Elvin Jellinek suggested that alcoholism involves five basic types
of alcohlics.[13] To simplify the classification, he used Greek letters:
alpha, beta, gamma, delta, and epsilon.

1. *Alpha*: This type of alcoholic relies on the effect of alcohol to boost morale, bolster self-confidence, or relieve emotional
pain. Alphas could be regarded as social drinkers except for the
fact that they often drink too much, at the wrong times, among
the wrong people and thereby tend to affront others. The Alpha
type does not loose control and can abstain when necessary. However, their drinking leads to family arguments, occasional absenteeism from work, and a drain on the family budget. Alpha drinkers
may develop into full-fledged Gamma alcohlics. Hence, they are
considered by many researchers to be "pre-alcoholics" and should
be treated accordingly.

2. *Beta*: This type of alcoholic gets sick. Betas do not become
addicted and they suffer no withdrawal symptoms if they stop
drinking in time. However, their nutritional habit of substituting
alcohol for necessary proteins, minerals, and vitamins leads to
medical complications, such as peripheral neuritis, cirrhosis, and
gastritis. When hospitalized, their ailments are all too often treated
without regard to the drinking habits that have caused them.

3. *Gamma*: These are the alcoholics who most frequently
need help from alcoholism clinics and organizations such as Alcoholics Anonymous. Their psychological dependence upon alcohol
has grown into a physical dependence. They have lost control over

their drinking and suffer withdrawal symptoms when they abstain. In the early and middle stages of the illness, their tolerance for alcohol is much greater than that of the nonalcoholic. In the late stages, however, their tolerance abruptly decreases to the point where even a single drink can make them ill.

4. *Delta*: Delta alcoholics maintain a steady concentration of alcohol in their bloodstream during waking hours. Usually, they have grown up in homes where alcohol is an all-purpose beverage, served at all meals. But they also can come from homes where eye-openers and the three-martini lunches have become a ritual or from "little-old-lady" drinking homes whose daily quota of a dry sherry is a must. Seldom visibly intoxicated, the Delta alcoholic will suffer withdrawal symptoms when forced to abstain.

5. *Epsilon*: This is the so-called binge drinker, who will perhaps go for a period of weeks, months, or even years without a drink. But once the drinking starts, it is explosive. Epsilon drinkers continue drinking until they collapse. If the binges continue with increasing frequency, they may become Gamma alcoholics.

Despite the protests of many alcoholics, particularly the gammas, deltas, and epsilons, that they "can take it or leave it" or "only drink on pay day," there is one common denominator: consciously or subconsciously, they are forever looking forward to and planning for that next drink whenever it may be. While Jellinek has described five major classifications of alcoholics, there are perhaps as many different subtypes as there are alcoholics. All, however, have one thing in common: excessive drinking.

Two defenses that alcoholics commonly use are *rationalization* and *projection*. A rationalization is an intellectual defense that will excuse many forms of behavior and concurrently prevent emotional punishment. Thus, the alcoholic will give many reasons for drinking excessively, none of which places him or her in a bad light. Projection is the process of shifting self-hatred to others. The more hateful alcoholics unconsciously see themselves to be, the more they will come to see themselves surrounded by hateful people. It should be remembered that both of these defenses are unconscious. These defenses lock in the alcoholic's negative feelings and create a condition of unresolved anxiety, guilt, shame, and remorse.

PREADDICTION. The road to alcoholism begins when drinking is no longer social but a means of psychological escape from tensions and inhibitions. Initially, this type of drinker is in reasonable control. However, heavy drinkers begin to fall into a definite pattern:

1. *Gross drinking behavior*: They begin to drink more heavily and more often than their friends. "Getting high" becomes a habit. When drunk, they may develop a "big shot" complex, recklessly spending money and boasting of real and imagined accomplishments.

2. *Blackouts*: A "blackout," or temporary loss of memory, is not to be confused with "passing out," which is a loss of consciousness. Drinkers suffering from a blackout cannot remember things they said, things they did, or places they visited. It is important to note that even a social drinker can have a blackout. With prospective alcoholics, blackouts are more frequent and develop into a pattern.

3. *Gulping and sneaking drinks*: Anxious to maintain a euphoric level, they begin to drink heavily at parties and slyly gulp down extra ones when they think nobody is looking. They also may "fortify" themselves before going to a party to help along their euphoria. Ultimately, they begin to feel guilty about this behavior and avoid talking about alcohol or drinking.

4. *Chronic hangovers*: As they become more and more reliant on alcohol as a stress reliever, "morning after" hangovers become more frequent and increasingly painful.

ADDICTION. Until now, the problem drinker has been drinking heavily but not always conspicuously. More importantly, he or she has been able to stop drinking, but not now. At this point, he or she develops the symptoms of addiction with increased rapidity.

1. *Loss of control*: This is the problem drinkers' most common sign that their habit has become an addiction. They still may refuse to accept a drink, but once they take one they cannot stop. A single drink is likely to trigger a chain reaction that will continue without a break until a state of complete intoxication is achieved.

2. *The alibi system*: Their loss of control induces feelings of guilt and shame, so they utilize an elaborate system of "reasons"

for their drinking: "I just completed my assignment," or "I failed to complete my assignment," and so forth. While hoping their excuses will justify their behavior in the eyes of their family and associates, in reality they are mostly to reassure the alcoholics.

3. *Eye-openers*: They need a drink in the morning "to start the day off right." An eye-opener is in fact sedation to ease the trauma of facing reality.

4. *Changing the pattern*: By now they are under pressure from their family, employer, or both. At this point, alcoholics will try to break the hold alcohol has on them. At first, they may try changing brands of alcohol. Of course, this does no good. Then they will set up their own rules governing when to drink (e.g. on weekends and holidays). They may even "go on the wagon" for a period, but one sip of alcohol and the chain reaction starts all over again.

5. *Antisocial behavior:* Alcoholics begin drinking alone or only with other alcoholics, regardless of their social class. They believe that only other "drinkers" can understand them. Many alcoholics complain about imagined wrongs inflicted by others outside their drinking world. They think people are staring at them or talking about them. Finally, they become highly critical of others and may even become physically aggressive.

6. *Loss of friends and jobs:* Their continuing antisocial behavior causes the alcoholics' friends to avoid them; their spouses leave them. The same situation develops with employers and fellow workers.

7. *Seeking medical aid*: The physical and mental pain caused by uncontrolled drinking may lead them to seek medical and/or psychiatric relief, but because they will not admit the extent of their drinking, they seldom receive any lasting relief. Even when they do admit their addiction, they do not adhere to a medical regimen.

LAST STAGE. Until they have reached this point, alcoholics have a choice – whether or not to take the first drink. In this last stage of alcoholism, they have no choice – they must drink.

1. *Benders*: They get "falling down" drunk for several days at a time, hopelessly searching for the feeling of alcoholic euphoria they once knew. They totally disregard everything – family, job,

food, even shelter. These periodic flights into oblivion could be called "drinking to escape the problems caused by drinking."

2. *Tremors*: In the past, their hands trembled a bit on mornings after being drunk, but now they get "the shakes" during periods of abstention. Tremors rack the whole body. Combined with hallucinations, they are known as *delirium tremens* (the DTs), which are fatal if medical help is not received. During and immediately after a tremor attack, most alcoholics vow to stop drinking.

3. *Protecting the supply*: Having an immediate supply of alcohol available becomes the most important thing in these alcoholics' lives. They spend their last money and, if necessary, will steal or sell themselves to get more alcohol. They hide their bottles so there will always be a drink close at hand when they need it, which can be anytime of the day or night.

4. *Unreasonable resentments*: They become increasingly more hostile to others. This frequently is a conscious effort to protect their precious liquor supply, which is hidden in places where they live and work.

5. *Nameless fears and anxieties*: They become constantly fearful of things they cannot see or describe in words. This feeling of impending doom or destruction adds to their stress and the compulsion to drink. These fears frequently appear in the form of hallucinations, both auditory and visual.

6. *Collapse of the alibi system*: They finally realize that they can no longer make excuses for their drinking or put the blame on others. It is painful to acknowledge that they have been fabricating lies to justify their drinking. The lies were preposterous to others and now are ridiculous to the alcoholic. Lies give way to the truth, which is that their drinking is beyond control.

7. *Surrender process*: Now or never, they must give up the idea of ever drinking again and must be willing to seek and accept help to make this possible. If an alcoholic is unable to stop drinking at this stage, his or her death is imminent. Death may come in advanced cases of cirrhosis of the liver, pancreatitis, or hemorrhaging of the esophagus. Or it may come from suicide. At various times in our nation's history, alcohol has been called a wonder drug. Since the discovery of distilled alcohol, scientists have discovered many other drugs more efficient at deadening pain than

alcohol. Even so, alcohol is still a wonder drug: alcoholics wonder where they have been; they wonder where their money has gone; they wonder where their friends have gone; and they wonder where their family has gone.

In 1957, the Community Services Committee of the AFL–CIO issued a pamphlet that succinctly summarizes several points I have been trying to make:

> [The alcoholic] is a sick person. He can no more control his compulsion to drink than a diabetic can control his reaction to sugar. When he sobers up, the alcoholic intends to stay sober. But a single drink can start him on the same downward spiral. . . .
> The alcoholic is not necessarily a weak-willed person. In most cases he is a compulsive drinker; once he takes his first drink he can't stop drinking, no matter what the consequences to himself, his family, his friends or his job. The majority of alcoholics are not "skid-row" types. They are not found in the Monday morning court line-up, or wandering dazed and shocked through back streets, or discovered in the emergency ward of the city hospital. Quite the contrary.
> Over 85 percent of them on the surface lead normal lives, have homes and families, are employable and usually working. They often have exceptional skills.
> Alcoholics do not represent any single group in our population. They are professional people, government officials, tradesmen, executives, skilled craftsmen, and workers. Like all diseases, alcoholism cuts across all lines, reaches all segments of society.[14]

Special Programs

Few agencies have formal written policies or procedures for dealing with alcoholism and drug abuse. In order to develop a sound recovery program, it is important to build on the foundation of a clearly written policy statement that has been developed and agreed to by the workers. A written policy should serve the following purposes: first, it should not leave to improvisation the purposes, nature, and benefits of such a program; second, it should have procedures to be followed in implementing the policy, and it should be a guide for the uniform administration of all elements of the program; third, it should should encourage the workers' voluntary utilization of the program through assurances of confidentiality, job security, insurance coverage, and acceptance of the disease concept of alcoholism; and fourth, it should serve as a training tool for all agency personnel involved in implementing the policy. Lewis Preshall listed the following characteristics of a good alcohol-recovery policy:

1. A definition of what the company regards as alcoholism, as distinct from social drinking. This should be a pragmatic, rather than a technical definition; something like, 'An employee will be considered to have alcoholism when his drinking seriously and continuously interferes with any major part of his life, such as his job, his health or his family.'
2. A statement that the company will give assistance in finding adequate treatment to any employee with alcoholism who wishes help with his drinking problem.
3. A statement that if all reasonable efforts at treatment fail, or if the employee consistently refuses to seek treatment, and if his drinking continues to interfere with his work performance, appropriate disciplinary action will be taken according to existing procedures.[15]

It is important that the program covers everyone. No employee or class of employees enjoys special immunity to alcoholism. The objectives of the agency are to assist the individual to arrest the disease and be restored to full health and a rewarding productive life. When alcoholism is diagnosed and treated as a disease by organization programs, the results have been successful for the majority of employees. Preshall cautioned:

One other word should be said about the application of discipline. It is especially important that the dividing line between discipline for violation of company rules and the treatment process be kept firmly separate, except in terms of motivation. A person with alcoholism should never be disciplined just because he has alcoholism. He should never be terminated or disciplined merely because it comes to management's attention that he has alcoholism. We do not discipline employees for having an illness. We may have to apply discipline if they refuse to seek medical attention and *if their work performance continues to suffer* as a result of the illness. In the long run, a company will probably terminate some employees after an alcoholism program has been in effect for a year or two. Such terminations will occur for one of three reasons: (1) violation of work rules, (2) continued unwillingness to seek treatment for alcoholism after reasonable effort to encourage treatment has been made by the company, or (3) failure to respond to treatment after every available therapy has been tried.[16]

Perhaps the most successful treatment program is Alcoholics Anonymous. It is a fellowship of men and women who have the common problem of alcoholism. They support each other in their sobriety by following a simple twelve-step program. Members attend meetings on an anonymous basis, using only their first names. Open meetings can be attended by anyone and are open to the public, while closed meetings are for alcoholics only. Membership is open to any alcoholic who wishes to overcome alcoholism and there are no dues.

Other resources include long-term and short-term treatment centers located in hospitals, mental health centers, and special drug facilities. Also not to be overlooked is the contribution of religious leaders trained as alcoholism counselors. The spiritual recovery of the alcoholic is an integral aspect of a successful rehabilitation program.

Henry Guntrip succinctly captured the fear of many nonalcoholics who find themselves helping alcoholics: "Is what I am seeing really in him or is it in me; or if it is really in him, does it affect me so much because it is in me also? I am a group of different persons, seeing and reacting to you who also seem to be a group of different persons, some of whom are probably really in you and others of whom I project into you."[17]

Techniques and Tips

One of the first signs of alcoholism may be a deterioration of job performance. The alcoholic becomes afraid that people are going to notice his or her drinking problem. So, rather than look for deterioration in job performance, it would be more productive to look for changes in work performance. This does not mean that every person who has a change in work performance is an alcoholic, but a supervisor should investigate any change in work performance.

Another clue is the "morning after" look, which most commonly occurs after extended periods from work (weekends, whole days, etc.). Red eyes and looking like the individual has not had much sleep may be important signs. Alcoholics seem to get sick more often than other workers. They have upset stomachs, headaches, and medical problems that most other groups of people don't have as regularly. These become excuses for not going to work. By directing these workers to seek medical help, the supervisor is exercising good judgment. If the workers have non-alcohol-related illnesses, they will get competent medical help. If they have alcohol-related problems, the supervisor can help them to get treatment and rehabilitation.

Most alcoholics have cash flow problems. Drinking costs money. Even beer drinkers get in debt. Approximately 40 percent of the alcoholics treated in the United States are strictly beer drinkers, so supervisors should not succumb to the old myth that you cannot become an alcoholic on beer. Letters of indebtedness and bad checks sent to a worker's employer may be a sign of alcoholism.

Marital difficulties frequently are the result of excessive drinking by one or both parties. Many times alcoholics will say, "I drink because I'm having trouble at home." Seldom do they say, "I have trouble at home because I drink." Most spouses corroborate their alcoholic mate's stories. It is difficult to expose a loved one's alcoholism. Besides, there is the fear that to do so will cost the family income and social status.

Other signs include the frequent odor of alcohol on a worker's breath, automobile accidents, excessive drinking at agency and other social functions, and consistently early departures from work. Any of these signs could denote a drinking problem, but none of them necessarily does. The message I am giving here is, Do not jump to unwarrented conclusions. An individual who exhibits several of the preceding behaviors or symptoms is likely to have a drinking problem.

It is crucial that the persons close to the alcoholic understand the nature of his or her problem. They must take the initiative if the illness is to be arrested. Colleagues are justifiably fearful of unpleasant confrontations, and this is exactly what will occur when an alcoholic is confronted. Alcoholics view any attempt to interrupt their drinking or change their life-style as meddling. This is one of the most baffling symptoms of alcoholism. Alcoholics refuse to admit that they have a problem and anyone suggesting that they do is meddling. Even when their jobs are threatened, when everyone in the agency is aware that they are in deep trouble, when their health, family, and sanity are slipping away, many alcoholics will still manage to cry out indignantly, "What do you mean? I don't have a drinking problem!" Rationalization, projection, and denial make it impossible for alcohlics to understand or accept their drinking problem. After the supervisor decides to intervene and confront an individual, he or she should be sure that:

1. *Significant other persons present the facts or data.* They must be individuals who can and do exert influence on the alcoholic. The interveners who appear to have the most success are employers or colleagues at the next higher level above the alcoholic.

2. *The data presented is specific and descriptive of events that have happened or conditions that exist.* When presenting data, don't be apologetic and don't exaggerate or minimize the facts (i.e. "I was there when you insulted the client, and it was obvious to both the client and me that you had been drinking." Opinions such as "I think you have been drinking too much" are useless and only raise the defenses of the alcoholic). The more facts the better, but they should show concern rather than being judgmental. Nor should you moralize or lecture the alcoholic.

3. *Available choices acceptable to the intervener are offered.* A good approach is: "You can go to this treatment center, that hospital, or Alcoholics Anonymous. Which help will you choose?" Remember, the problem and the decision are the alcoholic's. Do not assume responsibility for the alcoholic worker's success or failure. You are there to help, but the solution to the problem rests primarily with the alcoholic.

EXERCISE DRILL

Signs of Alcoholism*

The following questions will help you to learn if you or a colleague have some of the symptoms of alcoholism. Check the appropriate answer:

---

*National Council on Alcoholism, 733 Third Avenue, New York, N.Y., 10017.

Yes   No

1. Do you occasionally drink heavily after a disappointment or a quarrel or when the boss gives you a hard time? ___ ___

2. When you have trouble or feel under pressure, do you always drink more heavily than usual? ___ ___

3. Have you noticed that you are able to handle more liquor than you did when you were first drinking? ___ ___

4. Did you ever wake up on the "morning after" and discover that you could not remember part of the evening before, even though your friends tell you that you did not "pass out"? ___ ___

5. When drinking with other people, do you try to have a few extra drinks when others will not know it? ___ ___

6. Are there certain occasions when you feel uncomfortable if alcohol is not available? ___ ___

7. Have you recently noticed that when you begin drinking you are in more of a hurry to get the first drink than you used to be? ___ ___

8. Do you sometimes feel a little guilty about your drinking? ___ ___

9. Are you secretly irritated when your family and friends discuss your drinking? ___ ___

10. Have you recently noticed an increase in the frequency of your memory "blackouts"? ___ ___

11. Do you often find that you wish to continue drinking after your friends say they have had enough? ___ ___

12. Do you usually have a reason for the occasions when you drink heavily? ___ ___

13. When you are sober, do you often regret things you have said or done? ___ ___

Yes No

14. Have you tried switching brands or following different plans for controlling your drinking? ___ ___

15. Have you often failed to keep the promises you have made to yourself about controlling or cutting down on your drinking? ___ ___

16. Have you ever tried to control your drinking by making a change in jobs or moving to a new location? ___ ___

17. Do you try to avoid family or close friends while you are drinking? ___ ___

18. Are you having an increasing number of financial and work problems? ___ ___

19. Do more people seem to be treating you unfairly without good reason? ___ ___

20. Do you eat very little or irregularly when you are drinking? ___ ___

21. Do you sometimes have the "shakes" in the morning and find that it helps to have a little drink? ___ ___

22. Have you recently noticed that you cannot drink as much as you once did? ___ ___

23. Do you sometimes stay drunk for several days at a time? ___ ___

24. Do you sometimes feel very depressed and wonder whether life is worth living? ___ ___

25. Sometimes after periods of drinking, do you see or hear things that aren't there? ___ ___

26. Do you get terribly frightened after you have been drinking heavily? ___ ___

If you answered "yes" to any of the questions, you have some of the symptoms that may indicate alcoholism.

"Yes" answers to several of the questions indicate the following stages of alcoholism:

Questions 1–8 – Early Stage
Questions 9–21 – Middle Stage
Questions 21–26 – The beginning of the Final Stage

REFERENCES

1. Quoted in Institute on Alcohol Abuse and Alcoholism: *Alcohol and Alcoholism: Problems, Programs, and Progress.* Washington, D.C.: U.S. Government Printing Office, 1972, p. 3.
2. "Alcoholism," *Collier's Encyclopedia,* 1976 ed.
3. Alcoholism Center: *Handbook for the Alcoholism Counselor.* Baltimore, MD: Baltimore City Health Department, 1972, p. 5.
4. Ibid.
5. Ibid.
6. Johnson, V.E.: *I'll Quit Tomorrow.* New York: Harper & Row, 1980, p. 1.
7. Brisolara, A.: *The Alcoholic Employee.* New York: Human Sciences Press, 1979, p. 160.
8. Ibid., p. 161.
9. Ibid., p. 162.
10. Fox, R.: *What Can Be Done About Alcoholism.* New York: National Council on Alcoholism, 1959, pp. 1-2.
11. Armor, D.: *Alcoholism and Treatment.* New York: John Wiley & Sons, 1978, p. 28.
12. See Sharon W. Rohner: Alcoholics in the helping professions: Helping one another. *Alcohol Health and Research World,* 6:18, 1982.
13. Jellinek, E.M.: *The Defense Concept of Alcoholism.* New Haven, CT: College and University Press, 1968, pp. 60-65.
14. AFL-CIO Community Services Committee: *What Every Worker Should Know About Alcoholism.* Quoted in Jellinek, Ibid., p. 180.
15. Preshall, L.F.: "Alcoholism – An Employee Health Problem." Address delivered at the Ninth Annual Pacific Northwest Occupational Health Conference, Portland, Oregon, September 10, 1962.
16. Ibid.
17. Guntrip, H.: *Mental Pain and the Curse of Souls.* London: Independent Press, 1964, pp. 65–66.

Chapter 6
MENTALLY ILL

LIKE all people, when human service personnel experience conditions of stress, it is natural for them to use defense mechanisms—repression, suppression, rationalization, projection, compensation, substitution, reaction formation, sublimation, fantasy, regression, negativism, somatic reactions, and identification. These become *coping mechanisms* that allow an individual to adjust to problems. The survival of a worker is dependent on being able to regulate personal feelings, beliefs, and actions so that anxiety remains at a manageable level.

While defense mechanisms do not in themselves solve problems, they may allow an individual time to cope with them until better solutions are found. When defense mechanisms cease to relieve stress, workers turn to behavior that is called "maladjustment" or "maladaptive." But a few words of caution are in order: there is a thin line between normal behavior and neurotic and psychotic behavior. Except for extreme psychosis, what is normal and what is abnormal are difficult to ascertain. Besides, most normal people have periods of maladjustive behavior, and most maladjusted people have periods of rational behavior. Borderline personality types exhibit the following behavior:

1. *Belligerence.* Walking around continuously with a chip on the shoulder, ready to argue or quarrel at the slightest excuse, or even without an excuse.
2. *Excessive moodiness.* Spells of blues, or feeling down in the dumps; feeling a great deal of the time that nothing is worthwhile or really matters.
3. *Exaggerated worry.* Continuous anxiety about nothing at all or entirely out of proportion to the cause.

4. *Suspiciousness and mistrust.* A persistent feeling that the world is full of dishonest, conniving people; that everyone is trying to take advantage of me.

5. *Selfishness and greediness.* Lack of consideration of the needs of others; a "what's-in-it-for-me" attitude about almost everything.

6. *Helplessness and dependency.* A tendency to let others carry the burden; difficulty in making decisions.

7. *Poor emotional control.* Exaggerated emotional outbursts out of proportion to the cause and at inappropriate times.

8. *Daydreaming and fantasy.* Spending a good part of the time imagining how things could be, rather than dealing with them the way they are.

9. *Hypochondria.* Worrying a great deal of the time about minor physical ailments; experiencing imaginary symptoms of illness.[1]

Workers characterized by behaviors reflecting conditions of despair, loneliness, and cynicism are *alienated.* The anomic aspects of human service alienation are fourfold. The individual worker believes that (1) community leaders are indifferent to and detached from his/her needs, (2) human service work conditions are getting progressively worse, (3) life is meaningless, and (4) his or her immediate circle of friends is not supportive. The life themes of alienated workers include a preference for *fatalism* and an *orientation to the present.* Feeling helpless in an unpredictable world, these workers resort to a "live for today" philosophy that leaves little room for projecting long-range goals. Dropping out of human service work or getting another job seems to make more sense to them. This is but another way of running from reality. Some workers merely "go crazy."

Definitions

Any discussion of mental illness requires an understanding of mental health as well. The word *health* comes from the Anglo-Saxon root "hal," which means both whole and holy. In *Born to Win,* Muriel James describes whole or healthy persons as ones who experience a sense of harmony: "their bodies, minds and spirits tend toward integration as well as individuation."[2] Thus, in transactional analysis theory, mental health is synonymous with *autonomy.* This means being self-governing, determining one's destiny, taking responsibility for one's own actions and feelings, and adopting socially appropriate behavior.[3] One of the earliest recorded views of mental illness is in the Old Testament. Jews who failed to keep the commandments were punished with madness: "The Lord shall smite thee with madness. . . " (Deuteronomy 28:28). Obedience to the law was normal behavior.

The Greek philosopher Plato developed a concept of normality four thousand years before Christ. He divided the human soul into the rational and the irrational. The rational soul was the rightful leader; it was located in the brain, and its outstanding features were immortality and divinity. The irrational soul was mortal, and from it came all the "base emotions" of which humankind is capable.

In Plato's system, mental illness resulted when the irrational soul evaded the leadership of the rational soul. He described three kinds of "madness"—melancholia, dementia, and mania—all of which he thought were products of this disunion of the rational and irrational souls. Indeed, Plato's rational and irrational souls bear a strong resemblance to Sigmund Freud's rational *ego* and irrational *id*.[4] For our purposes, normality has the following characteristics: (1) absence of mental disease, (2) socially acceptable adjustment to the environment, (3) consistency in personality, and (4) correct perception of reality.

Mental illness has many forms, degrees of severity, and symptoms. These illnesses vary not only among individuals but within the individual over time. There is never a complete cure and always the possibility of a relapse or even a different form of illness. No person or group is exempt from the possibility of mental illness, and predictability is very low. As Robert Noland stated:

> While there are many symptoms of mental illness, deficiency, and defects, the simplest and most pragmatic indications are that in mild cases the sufferer simply cannot learn or is chronically unhappy and insecure; in more acute cases he is unable to adapt successfully to his environment, and in very acute cases he loses contact to some degree with reality. Under such circumstances he lives in an unreal world of fantasy and fear. In consequence, his perception of reality becomes faulty: He sees and hears things which do not exist or fails to perceive things in his environment, or what he sees and hears he misinterprets. His behavior often becomes bizarre and inappropriate, dangerously uninhibited or excessively withdrawn and inhibited. . . .

The result, whether the defect or illness is mild or acute, is a basic inability to adjust or a progressive deterioration of judgment and common sense. It is for this latter reason that *there is no necessary cor-
relation between intelligence as measured by tests and judgment.*[5]

One of the more serious characteristics of mental illness is that it
affects the workers' value systems, i.e. their sense of right and
wrong. Because values are personal and emotionally based, they
are always considered by the individual to be correct and true even
when they are in conflict within the individual. In the agency setting, this can lead to disastrous results for both the worker and his
or her clients.

Another form of mental illness is senility. Senility is most
common among the aged and manifests itself gradually. Although
the individual does not forget what he or she has already learned,
it becomes increasingly more difficult to assimilate new knowledge
and acquire new skills. As the process of deterioration continues,
it becomes increasingly similar to alcoholic intoxication. "The significance of senility lies in the fact that cerebral arteriosclerosis,
other circulatory disturbances, and senile brain disease account for
26 percent of all first admissions to mental hospitals. When allow-
ance is made for the fact that only the seriously deteriorated are
committed, it may be seen that the incidence of this disorder
among the elderly is very great."[6]

BASIC DATA. The scope and magnitude of mental illness in
the United States can only be estimated. A commonly accepted
figure is that 10 percent of the population, roughly 20 million
people, are currently suffering from some type of mental illness.
Of every two hospital beds in the United States, slightly more than
one is being used by a mental patient. Of all persons going to general hospitals for physical ailments yearly, it is estimated that 6
million are suffering from some form of mental illness that is partially responsible for their physical problems. There are probably
as many as 8 million individuals with severe mental and emotional
illness who have never been detected or diagnosed (i.e. cranks,
crackpots, eccentrics and fanatics, recluses, the antisocial, rebels
without causes, and the hypersuspicious). Cases of juvenile delinquency, alcohol and narcotics addiction, suicide, and other socially disruptive behavior are often symptomatic of mental illness.[7]

Leo Levy and Louis Rowitz studied admissions to Chicago in-patient psychiatric facilities over a one-year period and found that no group was more likely than any other group to suffer from mental illness.[8] The exception was old persons, and there is certain justification in the belief that this is not due to a greater incidence of mental illness but to the American negative attitude toward aging persons. Levy and Rowitz's observations are generalizable in the following way: by age, persons under twenty-five are under-represented and persons over sixty-five are overrepresented. Male admissions exceed female admissions; while most male admissions come from the lower socioeconomic classes, female admissions have broader socioeconomic representation. Unmarried persons utilize mental hospitals more than married persons, and individuals who have never been married have the highest utilization of mental hospitals.

Poverty or residence in a socially disorganized area are more significant factors than race. The fact that nonwhite rates of hospitalization are somewhat lower than white rates appears to be related to a higher arrest and imprisonment rate for nonwhites than for whites for equivalent behavior. Blacks typically receive more severe psychiatric diagnosis than whites. There is little evidence that social class is linked to the number of incidences of mental illness, but the poor are more likely to use public facilities, to be more severly diagnosed, and to be readmitted.

Social change seems to be an important factor in mental illness. The breakdown of old communities, the break up of the family unit, changing social values, and a faster pace of life cause the suspension of established systems of social support and put debilitating pressure on individuals who otherwise might function successfully. Each of these factors brings certain pressures to bear on the workers. However, we do not know why some individuals successfully cope while others falter and fail.

The problem of mental illness is extremely complex. Approximately one-fifth of all employees will suffer from some degree of mental disorder. It is rare that a mentally ill individual is aware of his or her problem; therefore, he or she usually assumes that something is wrong with their job or the people around them. Anxiety and insecurity are common features in America, and tranquilizers are common "cures." In a society that is so strongly tied to its work ethic, it is not surprising that increasing demands for performance are put upon industry and social agencies.

Myths and Stereotypes

There still persists much misinformation about mental illness. A foremost, unfounded belief is that most mental diseases are due to brain damage. Few mental diseases are directly the product of brain damage. Most mental illnesses are caused by group interaction—sociopsychological and cultural processes. Holly Wilson and Carol Ren Kneisl list the following myths and stereotypes:

"1. Most patients in mental hospitals are dangerous.
2. People who are mentally ill let their emotions control them.
3. If parents loved their children more, there would be less mental illness.
4. When a person has a worry it is best not to think about it.
5. Many people would not become mentally ill if they avoided bad thoughts.
6. A woman would be foolish to marry a man who had a mental illness.
7. To become a mental patient is to become a failure in life.
8. One of the main causes of mental illness is the lack of mental strength."[9]

Contrary to popular opinion, we cannot tell who is mentally ill by observing behavior. Many ill persons are able to hide their disorders. Some are so adroit at their deception that they can get normal persons to question their own mental health.

Another misconception is that most mental illness is dysfunctional. It is not; most mental illness is functional. Functional mental illnesses involve no change in the brain even though it does not work properly. With help, individuals with functional illnesses can be restored to "normal" lives. Examples of mental illnesses of this type are drug and alcohol addiction. Workers can and often do recover without professional assistance, but whenever possible professional help should be utilized.

Severely maladjusted workers may be taking psychoactive drugs which are not completely harmless. Some drugs produce disturbing physical reactions such as rigidity of limbs, drooling, frequent urination, and increase in weight. Yet despite possible negative side effects, drugs are a valuable therapeutic tool. They do not cure psychiatric disorders, but they make it possible for psychotherapy to do so.

Nervous breakdown is not a scientific term. People embarrassed by friends or relatives who have mental illnesses frequently say that they have or had a nervous breakdown. The impreciseness of the term has caused it to connote any condition ranging from a mild behavior disorder to psychoses. Interestingly, some individuals with chronic physical disorders, such as arthritis, abscessed teeth, and appendicitis, may behave in ways to cause lay persons to label nervous breakdowns. In some subcultures, a psychotic person is believed to be "possessed by the devil or evil spirits." Along with this misconception, which has been perpetuated in movies and books, is the belief that all psychotic persons are dangerous. Actually, most of them are not.

The most insidious myth about mental illness is that it cannot be cured. If the illness is caught in time and proper treatment is given, 70 percent to 80 percent of all patients cannot only be released from treatment but they also can make a satisfactory adjustment to their environmental and interpersonal conditions.

Some persons still use the term *insane asylum* to designate an institution that cares for the mentally ill. "Asylum" means a place of refuge or security, but the old stereotypes of insane asylums were hardly refuges or secure places—they were damp, dark, dirty, crowded, noisy places where sick people were abused. Today's mental hospitals and homes are places of cure. There is less stigma attached to mental institutions than insane asylums. There are no "nuthouses," but there are people working in mental institutions who behave like Hollywood-script, nutty characters.

Finally, it is not true, as some uninformed people state, that once a person is cured he or she is always cured. There may be a reoccurrence of the illness or a new illness. This is not so much because the treatment was ineffective but because usually only an individual is treated, not his or her colleagues and family members who may be the cause or an aspect of the illness. "The central aim of 'therapy' — in cases in which full restitution is not possible —

appears to be to achieve transformation of the patient's personality in such a manner as *to enable him to make the right choice;* this choice must be capable of bringing about a new orientation, an orientation which is adequate enough to his nature to make life appear to be worth living again."[10]

Those Who Are Affected

In terms of work, there are three distinct groups among the mentally ill: (1) those who have developed emotional problems while working and are, therefore, in danger of leaving the work force; (2) those who have temporarily dropped out of the work force because of emotional problems but are able to return to work; and (3) the chronic mentally ill who have never worked, who have been absent from the work force for a long period of time, or who can no longer return to their former positions in the work force.[11] Of the three groups, the chronic mentally ill are the most difficult to place and retain within the work force. Fortunately, few human service workers are in this category.

Human service organizations are beginning to realize that they must face the problem of mental illness and help workers find ways of reducing, controlling, and coping with it. All organizations are composed of people and, therefore, all must cope with the emotional disorders of their workers.

In the past, counseling was used informally by supervisors to comfort a maladjusted employee. Stress was defined as a normal condition of work. In reality, some jobs are more stressful than others. When afflicted with extreme stress, some people improve, others get worse, and a few remain the same during their period of employment.

Many employees develop emotional problems while on the job. Some mentally ill employees actually show average or superior job performance, and, conversely, some emotionally well-adjusted employees do not function effectively because of work conditions or leadership styles. Ignoring job-related emotional problems does not solve them. Mental illness can be very costly for both the employer and the employee. Among the more common costs to the employer are:

1. Unnecessarily high labor turnover, excessive absenteeism, etc.
2. Substandard production.
3. Poor employee morale and internecine strife.
4. Poor public relations.
5. Excessive labor trouble.
6. Ill-advised company policies and practices often leading to the failure of the company (when top management is mentally ill or senile).

Among the costs to the employee are:

1. Chronic job dissatisfaction, with many changes of jobs.
2. Failure to achieve the goals that his intelligence, training, and experience merit.
3. Job tensions which create psychogenic disorders or lead to fight or flight symptoms (alcoholism, overeating, excessive smoking, etc.).[12]

Each worker's contact with reality is established through his or her perceptions. This definition of the situation is relative to each individual. W.I. Thomas once wrote, "If men define situations as being real, they are real in their consequences."[13] Thus, a false definition of the situation can become the "reality" that guides a worker's behavior. Obviously, if our perceptions are faulty, then our behavior will be distorted. Maladjusted workers attempt to restructure their job situations so that they can survive in it. Without understanding an individual's perceptions, we are poorly equipped to understand his or her responses.

A maladjusted worker displays a variety of distorted, defective patterns of thinking. An example of such thinking would be ideas stated without logical order, or starting a sentence without finishing it and moving on to another idea. Still other examples of distorted thinking would be irrelevance—what is said is logical but it has not relation to the current topic or activity. A worker may be asked, "Where is the folder for this client?" and he or she responds, "This place is too hot." Fragments of sentences come to disordered workers' minds and they feel compelled to say them. "Delusions, paranoid ideas, and obsessions are additional forms of disordered thinking. Delusions are false or improbable beliefs which have no relation to experience or reason. There are several kinds of delusions, such as delusions of having committed a crime, delusions of having an incurable disease, delusions of grandeur in which the person thinks he is wealthy or a great historical figure, delusions of worthlessness where he feels totally incompetent, and delusions of persecution where the individual feels something or someone is out to 'get' him."[14]

Delusions of persecution are a frequent maladjustment in workers who succumb to extreme stress. These workers are supersensitive, rigid, and humorless. They believe that no one in their agency likes them and that everyone is out to get them demoted or fired. These frightened people seem to have chips on their shoulders, as they argue or fight at the slightest imagined aggressive act. Needless to say, deluded workers have attitudes and behavior that make them difficult to work with. They become a prophecy of failure that fulfills itself.

Most human service workers are obsessed with helping their clients. This is disconcerting to friends who are subjected to endless conversations about the workers' problems on the job, but it is not dysfunctional. However, when thoughts of the job (or anything else) crowd out all other thoughts, they become major obsessions. A worker may realize how illogical it is to be obsessed in this latter manner but be unable to alter the situation. In the case of being obsessed with the job, these thoughts appear in working hours and during sleep, too.

There are several uncontrollable forms of behavior related to feelings and emotion that characterize a highly stressed worker. Some workers are hyperactive. They talk endlessly and badly. Some have uncontrollable temper tantrums that occur without external provocation. Still other workers develop phobias which cause them to avoid things that bother them. By now it should be clear that maladjusted behavior can be seen in a variety of symptoms. The most extreme disorders are neuroses and psychoses.

NEUROSES. The term *neurosis* means "full of nerves." The most common expression to describe a neurotic worker is that he or she had a nervous breakdown. But we should be careful in applying this term. The fact that someone is high-strung or tense does not necessarily mean that he or she is a neurotic. The symptoms I am talking about are one or more of the following: fear — ridden by unfounded dreads, obsessions and compulsions, unreasonable elation, constant depression, apathy, hypochondria, constant tiredness, loss of feeling of well-being, overwhelmed by daily activities, paralysis of the limbs, intense aches and pain, fits or seizures, tremors of the head and hands. Joseph Wolpe wrote: "The distress that the neurotic patient brings to the therapist for resolution is just as real and poignant as if it had been due to an organic illness. The most important criterion of therapeutic success is the lasting alleviation of this disturbance. It is of small comfort to a patient whose neurotic anxieties remain undiminished after treatment to tell him that he is cured because his personality has matured."[15]

The neurotic usually can function on the job and interact with people quite well. Because neurosis can take many forms, it is difficult to say in which areas a neurotic worker will not be able to perform. Some neurotic workers can perform well in some assignments and situations and not in others. It is when an individual breaks up mentally or physically and "goes to pieces" that we tend to worry. Neurotic workers frequently are aware of their condition and can intellectually discuss it. But awareness alone will not relieve their symptoms. Like psychoses, this disorder can become serious enough to require hospitalization.

PSYCHOSES. Unlike the neurotic, who while tense and unhappy is in control of his or her personality, the psychotic has lost control over his or her personality. The psychotic has lost contact with reality and requires close supervision. There are many symptoms, but for the sake of illustration I will mention a few: unable to communicate effectively, perceives the hands and feet to be smaller than usual, regression to infantile behavior, exalted hallucinations or delusions, fear that he or she will cease to exist, stupor, laughs and smiles inappropriately, and frequent crying spells. Psychotics occupy more hospital beds than any other type of patient. Thanks to advances in medical science, most of the new cases of psychoses and approximately one-third of the chronic cases can be treated and the client returned to work.

Special Programs

Changes in the mental health field have had a great effect not only on the treatment of the mentally ill but also upon the community at large. Until recently, most communities were able to insulate themselves and ignore the problems of the mentally ill. Whenever an individual's behavior became erratic enough to endanger or embarrass the community, he/she was committed to a hospital or prison to be cured. In this way society was protected and, as the reasoning went, the ill persons were relieved of social pressures and could heal in a quiet, sheltered environment. Numerous studies conducted in the 1950s and the early 1960s showed that this was not the case. Once institutionalized, it was highly unlikely that an individual would return as a productive member of society.

Hospital patients who adapted to an institutional setting, internalized its values and modes of behavior, accepted its cultural norms, and adjusted to its forms of social support were declared "cured" and released. After living in a mental institution and adjusting to its social systems, most patients were unprepared for the culture shock that they received upon reentering the larger society. Behavior that had been appropriate was no longer acceptable. Already stigmatized by having been institutionalized, the slightest deviations in behavior were enough to have the former patients reinstitutionalized. Thus we had a cycle of institutionalization, release, and reinstitutionalization.

The purpose of community mental health services is to allow the individual to remain in the community, be diagnosed and treated in the community, and thereby eliminate the problem of reintegration within the society. To as great an extent as possible, the mentally ill individual is not restricted in his or her mobility and social participation within the community. In this way, a worker's employer can assume an active role in his or her treatment and rehabilitation. As Sue Estroff states:

> Not only does deinstitutionalization represent a protest movement against the abuses and inefficiencies of institutionalization, but it sets in motion waves of change in service delivery and organizations in the entire mental health community. When I refer to community

treatment, it is as a part of these processes, in service to these values. In particular, I mean the diagnosis, treatment, and rehabilitation of persistently, severely disturbed members of a given population, among this same population. The major aims of this subset of community psychiatry are avoidance of psychiatric hospitalization and increased gratifying participation in social, vocational, and interpersonal activities of clients in the community.[16]

Community mental health systems have shown greater promise in helping workers who are going through mild or short-term periods of emotional disturbances. At some point, most people experience periods of maladjustment, mainly due to family problems, personal problems, and job-related stress. Sometimes human service workers do not know where to turn for help or cannot afford to pay for private psychiatric help. Community mental health systems provide a myriad of services and referral services at minimal cost or free for those who cannot afford to pay. What were once dozens of federal, state, county, community, and private agencies are now grouped within a system in which each of the links supports the others, thereby reducing redundancy or gaps in service. Once a worker gets over the personal embarrassment surrounding the admission of needing community help, he or she can effectively use these services.

The basic assumption behind community mental health systems is that the individual in an emotional crisis has many needs. As noted earlier, rarely is there one cause and one problem. Age, income, social status, family relationships, job pressures, race, alcohol or drug addiction, living situations, physical problems, educational level, and marital status are all variables that make each individual different and can compound his or her emotional problems.

AGENCY INVOLVEMENT. An organization that realizes that it has workers who are mentally ill is faced with an even greater problem: what can be done? The United States has a very large, expensive mental health industry that is only marginally successful in controlling mental illnesses. There is currently a great debate over an employer's obligation to the mentally ill. One view is that few agencies have the resources needed to deal effectively with such a massive problem and that their responsibilities lie in other areas rather than spreading their scarce resources to include a problem that only affects a small portion of their work force. The other extreme view is that only social agencies have sufficient professional resources to deal with the problem.

Robert McMurray stated that because mental illness is a great expense for public and private organizations, they should not become involved in the treatment of mentally ill employees but should instead turn their efforts toward stopping the spread of mental illness. He believes it is futile for agencies to try to change individual workers or alter their values. Instead, he proposed five steps for selection and placement of employees:

1. Careful selection of all new employees to exclude potential "problems."
2. Thoughtful placement of all employees (whether hired from the outside or promoted from within) to adapt their environments to them (the employees) rather than to force them to fit a job for which they are not suited.
3. The provision of sufficient job structure and strong, sympathetic, and supportive supervision to keep the employees' anxieties at a minimum. (There must be no ambiguity about the nature of their jobs, there must be a minimum of risk-taking decision making required, and supervision must provide additional structure and support.)
4. Insurance that there is a reasonable degree of *homogeneity of values* among employees at all levels to insure social cohesiveness and a minimal degree of conflict among employees and employee groups. (Value conflicts tend to lead to the exclusion of the individual from the society of his peers. This can be extremely threatening and anxiety provoking because it deprives the individual of the support and approbation of the members of his group.)
5. Provision of a *psychologically hygienic* job environment, i.e. one which offers:
   a. Tolerable working conditions.
   b. Acceptable security on the job. . . .
   c. Outlets for grievances and frustrations. . . .
   d. Adequate challenge.
   e. Recognition for superior performance.
   f. Periodic reviews of the employees' job performance (to let them know where they stand—thus minimizing their anxieties).
   g. Information at intervals about the company's business outlook (thus allaying anxieties about job security).[17]

Other authorities believe employers should become more actively involved in abating mental illness. This has led to the concept of *occupational mental health,* which is the concern for both the mentally ill employee and the factors that stimulate a mentally healthy climate in the work environment. As Alan McLean states: "Changes in our society have altered the ways in which people satisfy their economic, social, and psychological needs. They have required people to find new ways of obtaining job security, new social devices for protection against injury, sickness, and death, new modes of developing skills, forms of recreation, and sources of emotional support."[18]

The breakdown of the extended family, social class mobility, and the lack of geographical orientation (one-fourth of the American population moves annually) have all put greater pressures on organizations to provided job stability and security. It is commonly assumed that job satisfaction is related to mental health in our society.

The most important features of occupational psychiatry are that: (1) it deals with mentally ill individuals in the work environment without removing them from the work force; (2) it is concerned mainly with neuroses rather than psychoses, using psychotherapy rather than chemotherapy; and (3) it is primarily interested in proper handling of employees, training, and preventive research. The role of the occupational psychiatrist is very complex and varies according to the size, type, and nature of the organization. Robert Meineker suggested several areas in which a psychiatrist might be used as an internal resource. He or she can:

1. provide psychiatric consultation to troubled employees, augmented, as appropriate, by communication and clarification of their problems to management, their physicians, families, and other agencies for business, personal, medical, and family problems.
2. provide psychiatric consultation to management on matters relating to production efficiency of people at all levels in the company. Here the scope is broad and infinitely varied. Activities would include participation in selection, placement, transfer, promotion, separation, and retirement of employees, appraising those factors in the individual's personality which bear on his fitness or unfitness for work, clarifying his strengths and liabilities. The general effort should be to clarify both the manifest and latent content of problem situations so that the true motivations and relationships are apparent. Management would carry on from this point in making decisions.

3. provide psychiatric consultation to physicians in the medical department in situations where diagnosis is in question or treatment is hindered by untoward emotional attitudes.
4. promote and participate in the design and development of education programs at all levels of the company.
5. discover and help in the management of mental health problems in the company through observation of workers and working conditions, and following statistics dealing with absenteeism, turnover rates, accident rates, and efficiency rating.
6. maintain relations with other industries, public health departments, departments of labor, and management, educational, and research organizations on matters pertaining to occupational psychiatry.[19]

The discovery of new types of psychotropic drugs has reduced the need for long-term custodial care. In the last thirty years, approximately twenty new phenothiazines have been developed for the treatment of mental disorders. We can no longer justify hiding most of our mentally ill workers in isolated buildings. Regardless of the causes, a shift from hospital-based mental health services to community treatment has taken place in the mental health field.

Techniques and Tips

When dealing with the mentally ill or the mentally restored worker, we must take great care that our efforts do not further injure the worker. Mental illness is extremely complex, affecting no two individuals in the same way. *Only trained personnel should attempt counseling mentally ill workers.* There are a number of actions a supervisor can take and a number of mistakes that can be avoided to make it easier for the mentally ill or mentally restored worker to perform his or her job. First, realize that mental illness is a personal problem. The supervisor must be very careful not to meddle in the lives of his or her subordinates. Mental illness does not necessarily affect intelligence, skills, training, or the ability to learn. In cases of mild disorders, the worker is still an individual with a sense of humor, tastes and preferences, and a life outside of work. The supervisor should understand this and not take a paternal or maternal attitude.

Stress is a major factor in many forms of mental illness. No individual can work under high levels of stress over a long period of time without some adverse effects. A supervisor should understand the pressures of the job and the needs and capacities of the individual workers and try to achieve a healthy balance. Some general suggestions are:

1. Treat each employee as an individual.
2. Reduce stress whenever possible.
3. Do not pressure employees as a means of getting better results (often this only leads to greater problems).
4. Simplify jobs and procedures as much as possible, and explain the reasons behind all jobs and how they fit into the whole process.
5. Be open to questions and suggestions.
6. Give constructive criticism.
7. Fully explain all duties and responsibilities.
8. Be knowledgeable of agency programs and policies in dealing with mental illness and mental health.

It is important that organizations confront the issue of mental health. Depending upon the nature of the organization and its resources, some or all of the following actions can be taken.

1. Set a policy concerning the mental health of the members of the organization and guidelines for supervisors to follow.
2. If possible, provide employee counseling.
3. Understand that mental health is a form of health, and provide the same insurance coverage and benefits for it as for physical health problems.
4. Allow employees "mental health" days as part of their sick leave. Understand that stress is a real problem and can be crippling to the individual.
5. Look into alternative work scheduling programs for the possible beneficial effects they might have for the employees.
6. Look into alternative ways of structuring work for possible stress reduction, cross-training, and upward mobility.
7. Reduce bureaucracy, pettiness, and overemphasis on form and structure, and put more emphasis on the processes of interaction.

Throughout this chapter, I have been talking about caring for the mentally ill. What professional helpers can do to meet the needs of their colleagues who are mentally ill is questionable. It is abundantly clear, however, that such needs are being left unfulfilled in countless agencies. "The question of human relationships and of the inner cohesion of our society is an urgent one in view of the atomization of the pent-up mass man, whose personal relationships are underminded by general mistrust," Carl Jung wrote. "To counter this danger, the free society needs a bond of an affective nature, a principle of a kind like *caritas*, the Christian love of your neighbor. . . . Where love stops, power begins, and violence and terror."[20]

There is a belief that some people by nature can more easily care for the mentally ill than others. Although this is debatable, it does seem that some helpers are more willing than others to care for the mentally ill.

REFERENCES

1. Milt, H.: *How to Deal with Mental Problems.* New York: National Association of Mental Health, 1980, p.3.
2. James, M., and Jongeward, D.: *Born to Win: Transactional Analysis with Gestalt Experiments.* Reading, MA: Addison–Wesley, 1977, p. 55.
3. Berne, E.: *Games People Play.* New York: Penguin Books, 1964, p. 158.
4. For a critique of the psychoanalytic approach, see Dorothy Tennov: *Psychotherapy: The Hazardous Cure.* New York: Doubleday, 1976.
5. Noland, R.I.: *Industrial Mental Health and Employee Counseling.* New York: Behavioral Publications, 1973, pp. 4–5.
6. Ibid., p. 6.
7. Ibid., pp. 3–4.
8. Levy, L., and Rowitz, L.: *The Ecology of Mental Disorder.* New York: Behavioral Publications, 1978.
9. Wilson, H.S., and Kneisl, C.R.: *Psychiatric Nursing.* Menlo Park, CA: Addison–Wesley, 1979, p. 50.
10. Goldstein, K.: Health as value. In Maslow, A.H. (Ed.): *New Knowledge in Human Values.* Chicago: Henry Regnery, 1959, p. 182.
11. National Institute of Health: *The Mentally Restored and Work.* Washington, D.C.: U.S. Government Printing Office, 1981, p. 3.
12. Noland, *Industrial Mental Health*, pp. 9–10.
13. For a discussion of W.I. Thomas's theorem, see R.K. Merton: *Social Theory and Social Structure,* Glencoe, IL: Free Press, 1957, Chapt. 2.
14. Kaplan L.: *Foundations of Human Behavior.* New York: Harper & Row, 1965, p. 250.
15. Wolpe, J.: *The Practice of Behavior Therapy.* New York: Pergamon, 1973, p. 10.

16. Estroff, S.E.: *Making It Crazy*. Berkeley: University of California Press, 1981, p. 11.
17. Robert McMurray. In Noland, *Industrial Mental Health*, p. 22.
18. Alan McLean. In Noland, *Industrial Mental Health*, pp. 126–127.
19. Robert Meineker. In Noland, *Industrial Mental Health*, p. 214.
20. Jung, C.G.: *The Undiscovered Self*. New York: Mentor, 1957, pp. 117–118.

Chapter 7
OLDER WORKERS

AMERICAN business, government, social agency, and labor leaders have become concerned with the obvious but momentous fact that our nation is growing older. In 1980, the median age of our population passed 30 for the first time since World War II. That disclosure by the United States Census Bureau shattered the myth that the United States is still a youthful country.[1]

The recent history of older Americans is not a story of humane relations. Older people in America have by and large been separated from the mainstream of society, either by design or through neglect. Many of our social agency and industrial leaders seem convinced that older citizens cannot serve a useful purpose. Reflecting their own ages, these leaders are too impatient to let them try. Whatever the reason, a policy of neglect and disdain is shortsighted. This type of thinking ignores the fact that older people are the fastest growing segment of the population.

Definitions

Social gerontology is one of the youngest of the behavioral sciences. Most of the literature pertaining to the aged and the aging in the United States written before 1940 was devoted primarily to analyses of the biological processes of aging. Moreover, the studies that were made seem to have been conducted with a noticeable degree of nonchalance. The apparent casualness of the interest in aging can doubtless be explained largely by the fact that the average life expectancy for persons of either sex never exceeded 63.7 years until 1940. Today, the situation is quite different;

it is common knowledge that recent scientific advances have substantially increased the average life expectancy. After 1940, "the United States, like a woman who [had] just taken a good look in the mirror, [realized] that it [was] no longer as young as it used to be. The result [was] a feeling of shock followed by an earnest search for remedies to the creeping problems of age."[2]

The "search for remedies" had to be extended into new areas, since the very fact that the aged population had increased in size presented problems beyond the scope of biology. Gerontologists came to the realization that our society was not oriented toward solving these problems, which included such realities as the older person's need for employment, housing, and recreation. As Clark Tibbitts observed, "Our population has been oriented toward youth. Most of our attitudes and institutions have been developed with reference to an essentially young population. This has been particularly true of our employment practices, of our educational and recreational facilities, of the medical specialties, of social welfare services, and even of our religious institutions."[3] It was, then, in response to the need for new approaches to the problems of the aged that the science of social gerontology came into being.

Social researchers have hypothesized that the majority of older persons want to continue to be useful, participating, recognized, and wanted members of the community — in essence, to remain an integral part of society. They conclude that the fulfillment of this desire would be reflected in suitable living arrangements, physical comforts, financial security, emotional outlets, and companionship.

Other countries wonder why we ignore more than thirty million older persons at a time when we need the skills and knowledge that many of them have acquired and honed through the decades of tough, practical experience. It would seem that from a humanistic point of view, if not a capitalistic one, until now the benefits of America have been denied to those who helped make it possible. The international irony of the situation is most embarrassing.

The United States no longer has an under-thirty-years-of-age population and it is becoming increasingly older. Life expectancy in the United States has increased approximately ten years in the past three decades. Three-fourths of the population now lives to reach age sixty-five. But sixty-five is just the beginning. On the average, those who reach sixty-five live an additional fifteen more years. The increase in the number of older Americans is quite remarkable. Each day about three thousand Americans over sixty-five die, while four thousand enter that age group, for a total increase of nearly four hundred thousand annually. This aging population profile is not unique to the United States. Western Europe, Japan, and the communist countries are experiencing the same phenomenon. All industrial nations must deal with increasing numbers of older people who do not seem to fit very well into today's swift-paced, highly technological, youth-oriented culture.

In 1980, the United States Department of Health and Human Services, Administration on Aging, published a statistical analysis that examined the characteristics of "older workers" (those 45 years old and over) and trends in their participation in the labor force. The report stated that the employment patterns of older workers are expected to change significantly in the coming years. Tomorrow's older workers will be better educated and more skilled than those of today.[4]

The issue that few people discuss is *ageism*: "a process of systematic stereotyping of and discrimination against people because they are old—just as racism and sexism accomplish this with skin color and gender. . . . Ageism allows the younger generations to see older people as different from themselves. Thus they subtly cease to identify with their elders as human beings."[5]

Myths and Stereotypes

By stereotyping older people as inferior beings and discriminating against them, younger workers set in motion their own negative conditions in later life. Paraphrasing an old saying, The sins of the sons and the daughters accrue to the grandmothers and grandfathers. Contrary to the previously mentioned stereotype, most older workers are not only able to continue working but they are also extremely productive. The national trend is toward a longer, healthier life, toward more years with more energy, more ability, and more need to remain active. While it is true that most people want to enjoy at least partial retirement, few want to be forcibly, totally retired. In summary, a substantial number of older citizens are willing and eager to work.

There does not appear to be any way to grow old gracefully in the United States. Equally important, it is difficult for workers to grow old and remain useful. The old are not out of sight and, consequently, they are not out of the minds of younger workers. The encounter is daily. Less than 6 percent of our aged are in institutions. Within agencies, they stand in the way of the upwardly mobile. Outside agencies, they remind us of the final life cycle. In *As You Like It*, Shakespeare painted this literary portrait of growing old:

> The sixth age shifts
> Into the lean and striped pantelone
> With spectacles on nose and pouch on side;
> His youthful hose, well-sewed, a world too wide
> For his shrunk shank, and his manly voice
> Turning again to childish treble, pipes
> And whistles in his sound. Last seen of all,
> That ends this strange eventual history,
> Is second childishness, and mere oblivion,
> Sans teeth, sans eyes, sans taste, sans everything.

Contrary to popular opinion, our older workers as a whole are not useless persons. Movies and television specials perpetuate the image of our older citizens wasted to bones waiting to be buried. This is not to say that the elderly are without problems. They have many problems – many of them similar to younger workers'. Agency directors tend to be less empathetic toward older workers, preferring to see them retire rather than retrain or reduce their hours. Some of the myths and stereotypes pertaining to the aged are the beliefs that most old people are senile, mentally ill or in poor health, set in their ways and unable or unwilling to change, poor workers, isolated and lonely, have incomes below the official poverty level, are unable to have sexual intercourse, happy to retire from jobs and abandon the hassles of work, are hypochondriacs, and are basically alike.

Based on data pertaining to ethnic minorities, to be an old ethnic minority person is to be in double jeopardy. Along with the stereotypes about the ethnic group (e.g. shiftless, lazy, docile) are also added the stereotypes about growing old. The words to the old Negro spiritual "Nobody Knows The Trouble I've Seen" are certainly appropriate. Ethnic minorities do not live as well as non-minorities, nor do they live as long.

Although studies conducted by the United States Bureau of Labor Statistics in 1958–1959 and the New York State Division of Human Rights in 1972 both concluded that although differences in hourly output among age groups were insignificant, older workers suffered from the stereotypic notion that they are doddering, unproductive, inflexible, uninformed, and inactive.[7] This point of view is not only absurd but its effects can be tragic. Most majority-group Americans typically face job discrimination around age 45 (it is much earlier for ethnic minorities). Many are forced out of the work force in their middle sixties or earlier and are left to the questionable pleasures of a retirement that is too often devoid of personal challenges and frequently full of financial struggles. This kind of retirement definitely is not the "golden years" in the storybook dreams of most people.

Those Who Are Affected

A generation ago, seven out of ten American workers were men and fathers of families. As a rule, their wives did not work outside the home, and they had one or more children living at home. This was the classic *nuclear family*. The pool of the labor force was determined to be white males, and jobs were designed to meet the needs of these workers.[8] They were the "traditional" workers. In 1980, the traditional workers were but 15 percent of the labor force. They were sharing jobs with working wives, single parents, husband and wife teams, minorities, and others. Business, government, and public agencies were quick to accommodate this change.

Almost 70 percent of American men aged 65 and over were gainfully employed or seeking employment in 1900. By 1980, both men and women over 65 represented 13 percent of the labor force. Unless the trend is reversed, the percentage will be even lower in the year 2000. The sheer numbers of people without jobs will be financially and socially staggering. We must, as R.O. Anderson states, "take them off the shelf."[10]

The "discard shelf" simply is not big enough to hold all of the discarded workers. Those who support our nation's social insurance programs—the employed workers—are buckling under the load of future generations. Never in the history of the Social Security Act have so many people depended on so few for their income. The program is not going to operate much longer unless something is done to ease the load. In 1935, when the Social Security Act passed, there were eleven adults in the labor force for each Social Security recipient. Today only six active workers support each retiree, and the situation is getting worse because of our increasing longevity and decreasing birth rate. This trend toward what is sometimes referred to as "intergenerational interdependence" affects the federal budget and, relatedly, each wage earner. The long-term viability of Social Security must be put on a fiscally sound footing. Many private and public sector employer pension plans are also close to being insolvent. Soon the unfunded liabilities of public and private pension programs may exceed the national debt. Retirement and specifically early retirement appears to be unrealistic.[11]

A 1979 Harris poll concluded that 46 percent of retired people would prefer to work part-time or full-time. This same poll indicated that 51 percent of younger workers, tomorrow's retirees, expressed the desire to work in some meaningful activity after they retire. It is widely accepted that work is therapeutic for older people who choose it. This is also good for business and the nation. The rewards older people get from working are both economic and psychic. Part-time work is needed to supplement pensions as savings are increasingly eroded by inflation. Work also fosters a sense of usefulness, of being involved, active, and needed. When businesses and agencies offer work opportunities to older persons, they supplement their own talents with a vast reservoir of skills, experience, knowledge, and past productivity. As the pool of younger workers grows smaller in the future, it clearly is in the self-interest of organizations to look to older workers for more than token help.[12]

In regards to America in general, the benefits of using older people will be multidimensional. Studies prepared for the 1981

White House Conference on Aging suggest that expanded employment of older workers will boost the entire United States economy. Some economists believe this would add to United States gross
national product by almost 4 percent over the next 24 years. In
terms of money, this economic growth could add approximately
$40 billion in 1980 dollars to federal, state, and local tax revenues
in the year 2005.[13]

COMMON CHARACTERISTICS. Many elderly workers exhib-
it a high level of *anxiety*. Fear, shame, and physical deterioration
add to the stress inherent in most work situations. *Hearing loss* is a
common phenomenon: almost one-third of the older workers experience this sensory loss. Fewer workers (15%–20%) experience
extreme visual problems. Older workers tend to be more cautious
than younger ones. Most of their errors are of omission rather than
commission. Afraid that mistakes may cost them pensions, promotion, or just plain praise, they are likely to do only what is required. Part of this is because many elderly workers develop an unrealistic perception of their supervisors. In psychiatric terms, this
is *transference*: they view supervisors as parents or children. In
either case, the elderly worker has an obsessive need not to disap-
point supervisors.

Loss is a persistent theme of the elderly. They lose bodily functions, friends and loved ones, employment, and often self-esteem.
Some even lose their memory of previous events. Perhaps the
greatest fear is that they will lose their minds and go crazy. Most
older workers do not seem obsessed with losing their lives, but almost all of them fear being alone at death.

But it is not merely older workers who are affected by their
aging and impending death: all persons who work with them are
also affected. The older worker is the conduit of all the problems
we have discussed—racism, burnout, sexism, alcoholism, mental
illness, and terminal illness. In many ways, how we care for our
older workers is a valuable clue of how we care for younger ones
with problems.

Both young and old people frequently are torn between the
desire on the one hand to stay with the familiar and on the other
hand to venture forth into new activities. *New experience* occurs
when individuals encounter something that, in part or in whole,

they have never faced before. Too, a new experience may be an old situation to which a new variable has been introduced – for example, minority groups who suddenly must adjust to newly achieved equal employment opportunities. The need for new experience is the antithesis of the wish for maintaining the status quo. New experience describes actions which disturb the status quo, such as the behavior of a man who takes a vacation, quits his job, or laughs at his girl friend's new dress. Experiences that are too radical are usually disturbing rather than stimulating. To be commercially successful, for example, a new piece of music, a novel, or a clothing style must ordinarily be the familiar but done over in a slightly different manner.

The need for *security* can be seen in all actions that contribute to keeping things as they are. Efforts to keep a job or retain one's youth are examples of wishes or motives for security. Most people tend to resist revolutionary changes. Most of the social history of the later Middle Ages is a chronicle of the efforts of a majority to prevent a minority from introducing novel inventions and methods. The history of early science is characterized by the struggle against conservatism. Even today, we cling tenaciously to old cultural norms, however willing we profess to be for change. To illustrate, most industries still have double promotion standards for older and younger workers, with older workers generally receiving fewer opportunities for supervisory positions. Much of human conservatism is traceable to the fact that once a reasonably effective pattern of behavior is learned, any change that makes that pattern less effective is psychologically or socially distressing.

We also have a need for *recognition* – the need to be acknowledged for an accomplishment. To fail to be recognized by people important to us is one of the most dreaded forms of punishment. For instance, a civic group may decide to recognize a retiring worker. They schedule a banquet in her honor and invite many people, including representatives of the press. No matter how elaborate the preparation of food and decorations and certificates of honor, if the invited guests do not attend the banquet, the retiree has not received recognition. In highly competitive organizations, a great amount of human action has no other objective than that of individuals trying to assert their superiority over their associates.

Members of competitive societies are, by conditioning, egoists, each trying to rise above the others. Generally, old age brings fewer successes.

Closely related to recognition is our need for *response* from members of our groups. Because we derive our definition of self from others, we need feedback from them to help us shape our behavior. The social self arises in interaction with other persons as we look at ourselves through their eyes. We feel happy or sad as we evoke praise or blame from those with whom we identify.

All individuals have the need to receive *affection*, which provides confirmation of their positive self-worth. This kind of reinforcement is the basis of healthy personalities. It is a simple but significant fact that all of us need affection from other people in order to develop and maintain healthy personalities. Yes, people do need people—young and old.

Special Programs

Public Law 95-256, commonly referred to as the 1978 amendments to the Age Discrimination in Employment Act (ADEA), rendered legally unenforceable most mandatory retirement policies for people up to age 70. This act also prohibits employers from discriminating against persons aged 40 through 70 in hiring, firing, promotions, compensation, and other conditions or privileges of employment. Interestingly, the previous mandatory retirement age of 65 as outlined in the original 1967 ADEA was arbitrarily selected by New Deal planners because this age was used in Otto Von Bismark's social welfare system in Germany in the nineteenth century. In fact, Congress accepted the age of 65 for retirement without even considering any other age or related factors. Public Law 95-256 reflected an awareness by Congress of changing economic and social conditions in the United States.[14]

The 1974 Employee Retirement Income Security Act (ERISA), although complicated and full of flaws, gives employees greater protection for their pension programs. Prior to ERISA, employees enrolled in private pension plans often lost their pensions, sometimes after decades of participation. Among the causes for such losses were job transfers, companies going out of business, and employers mismanaging the pension funds.[15]

The federal government and several state governments have almost completely abolished compulsory retirement before age 70 for their own employees. Finally, Social Security laws have been liberalized so that retired workers can earn a limited amount of money without losing benefits. Although all of these changes help, much more needs to be done. The fact still remains that too few people over 65 who want to work actually do work.

WORK-FORCE ANALYSIS. A work-force analysis could identify occupations with high concentrations of older workers and predict the consequences for an organization if large numbers of these workers retire en masse. In addition, the analysis could ascertain older workers' interest in delaying their retirement and determine preferred alternative work options. Organizations anticipating a high turnover of experienced workers or a shortage of employees with particular skills could develop formal retention and rehiring policies for older workers and retirees. All organizations should carefully weigh the costs of implementing such policies against the cost of hiring and training replacements for their older workers.[16]

PART-TIME WORK. When considering the alternative of part-time work for older employees, most organization budgets are restricted to a fixed number of positions. Program managers usually are prohibited from hiring two part-time workers to fill one full-time position without building a case of unique circumstances. One solution is to count the number of part-time workers on a prorated basis. Another factor that can be taken into consideration by employers interested in converting full-time jobs into equivalent part-time jobs is the difficulty in finding employees with similar skills. For this reason, social agencies must develop policies to encourage part-time workers to be recruited from within as well as outside the organizations. Indeed, a few organizations are experimenting with procedures allowing two persons to jointly apply for the same position (e.g. job sharing by married couples).

JOB TRANSFERS. Frequently, productive older employees who find their jobs too demanding retire early and look for work with different employers. Sometimes this is done because lateral job changes in the same organization are viewed as being demotions in the eyes of coworkers. It is important that employers recognize this problem and, as some are doing, develop opportunities for lateral transfers into newly created or restructured jobs with recognized status. This removes the stigma of demotions for older workers who change jobs. An example of this would be a social agency creating "emeritus" positions for older, highly valued workers who could continue working but in the role of agency consultants. Although such positions might be at a lower salary, they would connote elevated or special status which may alleviate the psychosocial problems accompanying reduced or different work loads.

Modifying work schedules and redesigning jobs are relatively new ideas. The mechanics of implementing alternative work options take time to develop and will not be worked out unless employers perceive an advantage in doing so.

RETIREMENT PLANNING. The more progressive organizations are assisting older workers to become aware of opportunities, if any, for alternative work options and their impact on retirement benefits. In organizations where work options are available, the information provided to employees usually includes an explanation of the financial impact of the alternatives on retirement benefits.[17] This is especially important, because many older workers who are interested in alternative work options wish to extend their work lives but not at a financial loss. Several organizations use pre-retirement seminars to stimulate workers' interest in alternatives to full retirement. If workers wait just before their retirement dates to participate in such seminars, it may be too late to seriously consider alternative work options. Therefore, some employers organize and encourage worker participation in pre-retirement seminars at least several years prior to retirement in order to allow sufficient time to evaluate several work arrangements as alternatives to full retirement.

ECONOMIC INCENTIVE PROGRAMS. Most pension regulations penalize older workers who utilize alternative work options with the same employer. For example, pension regulations often prohibit employees from drawing their pensions while still working for the same employer and, in some cases, even disallow working a post-retirement job in the same industry. In other instances, the rules governing pension benefits penalize workers interested in most alternative work options. For example, in some organizations if individuals were to work half time, it would take them two years to accumulate one additional year of service based on existing organization pension regulations. Additionally, there is a disincentive to work part-time when calculations for retirement benefits are based on an employee's average salary for the years immediately preceding retirement.

A method now being tried by some private organizations is a separate in-house entity that serves as a job shop or employment service. In essence, retirees are rehired as temporary employees, able to draw their pensions to supplement their wages, but they are ineligible for pension accrual or other fringe benefits. The public sector is adjusting pension regulations through legislative change. For example, modifications in the Kansas Public Employees Retirement System permit employees to retire at age sixty or later, draw their pensions, and be rehired into their former jobs or other jobs for which they are qualified. Also, the Wichita Public School System has taken advantage of similar legislative change provisions to encourage job sharing.

A growing number of organizations are exploring the feasibility of permitting older workers who want reduced work schedules to continue having their pension contributions calculated as though they were working full-time and earning full salaries. The San Francisco Unified School District has adopted such a plan, which has met with considerable success. In this case, part-time employees do not collect their pensions.

The slowness of American organizations to recognize problems unique to older workers is part of the reason we have so few carefully planned programs for older workers. It is anticlimactic to wait until people retire before designing retirement programs. The majority of older workers need pre-retirement programs.

Techniques and Tips

Every social organization may be viewed as a miniature society, having its own norms that affect the attitudes and behaviors of its members in various ways. Members of an organization are controlled by three kinds of influence: (1) the formal structure of the organization, (2) the informal structure and norms of the subgroups within the organization, and (3) the surrounding community.

It is an established fact that we learn values, attitudes, and behavior from our social environment. Whether these experiences are planned or just happen, they form our basis for accepting or rejecting other people. For this reason, attention must be paid to the quality of interactions within and outside a group, since the quality of interactions significantly affects the ease with which each member will function.

For those who want to prevent or abate problems growing out of old age, it is necessary to focus on the past, the present, and the future. The major emphasis, however, should be on immediate reality, i.e. what is occurring today, not what happened yesterday. Those who dwell exclusively on historical grievances, such as ethnic, age, or sex discrimination, are likely to become hardened, bitter people who see little hope in the present or the future. Those who spend most of their time dreaming of the future are likely to lose touch with reality. Ultimately, leaders of organizations must be able to design older-worker activities that are relevant for today and tomorrow.

The foremost goal of any older-worker program should be to aid each individual in realizing his or her optimum individual and organization growth. This goal necessarily includes freedom for individuals to express themselves as long as they do not infringe on the constitutional rights of others. Specifically, an older-worker program should point out to all employees that age differences are not valid reasons for rejecting others. They must become willing to live with and accept age differences.

Because we learn what we live, the major emphasis in an older-worker training program should be on living good human relations. Reading books about other people is not enough; we must become able to live with them. Interaction is the best way to find out about people. For example, well-read old and young employees who segregate themselves on the job are not likely to learn all they can about each other. Their knowledge of each other will probably remain grossly inadequate.

On the premise that good human relations are not only good business but also desirable business, many industries are implementing training programs designed to improve human relations. The following concepts form the foundation for understanding and working with older people:

1. Every older individual is the sum total of all his or her experiences (objective interactions and subjective feelings), and he or she behaves in terms of these experiences.
2. Every older individual is endowed with psychological drives toward health, growth, and adjustment.
3. Every older individual perceives and behaves in terms of his or her own needs for security, acceptance, achievement, and independence.
4. Every older individual is capable of solving most of his or her problems if he or she understands the problems and learns to use his or her own resources.

The more effective administrators are aware of the fact that situations, individuals, and goals change constantly. They realize that most older workers like to do things that they do well and are reluctant to undertake activities in which they perform poorly or which are unfamiliar to them. A fully employed person, for example, may not be against part-time work but simply unfamiliar with the benefits that may accrue to him or her.

It is extremely important for both supervisors and colleagues to remember that each older worker is different and should not be placed in ethnic, sex, or color packages. They differ in intellect, ambition, and response. Each must be encouraged to develop to the limit of his or her capacities, but more than encouragement is needed, especially for members of minority groups. Opportunities must also be provided for all people to achieve in accordance with their aspirations. In terms of personality, older workers tend to be one of the following:

1. *Hostile workers* resent authority, especially young supervisors. They must be dealt with firmly but fairly to confine their aggressiveness and channel their energies toward the organization's objectives. Of course, we sometimes mistakenly assume that the attitude of another person is hostile when in fact it is not. When in doubt, it is good to ask ("Are you angry about something?").
2. *Dependent workers* need firm guidance. If unchecked, their dependence will cause them to flounder until the supervisor can tell them how to control their behavior. Few organiza-

tions are prepared to provide the amount of supervision that extremely dependent employees need.

3. *Cooperative workers* function best when given an opportunity to participate fully in decision making. They can usually operate within a set policy and need little guidance or control.

4. *Individualists*, or "lone wolves," work best when left alone. However, the administrator should make sure that they are "on course" and not working at cross-purposes to the organization.

Every human being, regardless of his or her personality, responds in some manner to supervision. How we respond depends on the style of leadership. A man forced to do a job against his will is likely to become a problem worker. The nature of the task and its importance must be effectively communicated to those expected to carry it out. In-service training programs involving all members of a unit or team can improve work skills and individual attitudes.

The trend in administration is moving away from emphasis on achievement to emphasis on self-actualization, from self-control to self-expression, from independence to interdependence. In any kind of organization, effective leaders understand the various personality types among their followers. They must be flexible in order to vary techniques and approaches as each situation demands. The rules may not be flexible, but those who administer them should be.

EFFECTIVE COMMUNICATION. A slow and relaxed pace can do much to relieve an older worker's anxiety. However, this does not necessarily require the younger person to talk slower. "Just because I move slowly doesn't mean I think slowly," an elderly worker once said to me. It is important that older workers be treated with respect. To some older workers, words such as "old man" or "old lady" are as offensive as "boy" and "girl" are to many black Americans. The key to most human relations problems is effective communication.

Administrators and coworkers who refuse to listen to what others are saying miss opportunities for positive interaction. In this instance, they *hear* but they do not *listen*. At all times we must be alert for obstacles to good listening that may be caused by prejudice against the elderly speaker, whether it is caused by his or her age, dress, or basic beliefs. Effective communication systems do not just happen; they are created. Nor should quantity of communication automatically be equated with quality. Informal gatherings, staff meetings, and individual conferences are occasions when communications can be checked for accuracy. Whenever possible we should send messages that convey the thought "I'm OK, you're OK." When there are so many positive things that we can say about people, it is an act of gross insensitivity to send only negative messages. In summary, communicating with older workers is the same as communicating with other workers: it is hard work that requires constant monitoring and refining.

REFERENCES

1. Anderson, R.O.: Off the shelf: New opportunity for older Americans. *Aging and Work, 4*:203, 1981.
2. *The Economist*, April 12, 1960, p. 54.
3. Clark Tibbitts. Quoted in *Living in the Latter Years: A Conference on Old Age*. Huntington, W.V.: Marshall University, 1950, p. 1.
4. U.S. Department of Labor: *Employment and Training*. Washington, D.C.: U.S. Government Printing Office, 1981, p. 94.
5. Butler, R.N.: Successful aging. *Mental Health, 58*:11, 1974.
6. William Shakespeare set a tone that was followed by other writers.
7. Rhine, S.H.: *Older Workers and Retirement*. New York: The Conference Board, 1978, p. 204.
8. Anderson, Off the shelf, p. 207.
9. U.S. Department of Health and Human Services: *Facts about Older Americans, 1980-81*. Washington, D.C.: U.S. Government Printing Office, 1981.
10. Anderson, Off the shelf, p. 207.
11. Ibid.
12. Beach, M.H.: Business and the graying of America. *Aging and Work, 4*: 197-198, 1981.
13. Ibid.
14. Gertzog, G.: The 1978 amendments to the Age Discrimination Act and their impact on personnel administration. *Forum, 14*:83, 1980.
15. Rhine, S., *Older Workers*, pp. 17-18.
16. Anderson, S., and Weagant, R. (Eds.): *Retention of Older Persons in the Labor Force*. Chicago: The Forum Series, 1972.

17. Wallfesh, H.M.: *The Effects of Extending the Mandatory Retirement Age.* New York: AMACOM, 1977, p. 37.

Chapter 8
TERMINALLY ILL

REFLECTING our general feelings about dying, Dylan Thomas wrote: "Do not go gentle into that good night/Old age should burn and rave at the close of day/Rage, rage against the dying of the light."[1] If older persons should resist dying in this manner, then younger ones should be even more resentful. Literature, music, and poetry are filled with romantic and, in some instances, grim writings of death. Death and dying also have been popular subjects of songwriters. Some works treat death as a welcome part of living, but most of them deal with death as Dylan Thomas's *Do Not Go Gentle Into That Good Night,* as dark, fearful, and something to be fought with our last breath. In much the same way as their ancestors, modern Western societies consider death and dying taboo subjects, couched in superstition and ominousness. We persist in dealing only with our longed-for immortality rather than face the fact of our inevitable death.

Shunned, too, are individuals with terminal illnesses. As though their cancer or heart disease or other fatal illnesses are contagious, we tend to keep our distance from them, preferring that they be placed in institutions rather than allowing them to intrude on our already hectic working lives. Terminal illnesses only linger to remind us that there are great limits to our abilities to help people, including ourselves.

Definitions

The term *terminal illness* has been given a variety of definitions. Dictionaries define "terminal" as situated at or forming the end of something; final or concluding. Terminal illness has been similarly defined. Yet each researcher and study has a slightly different focus on the etiology of terminal illnesses. For the purpose of this chapter, the term terminal illness will refer to a *variety of illnesses that have been diagnosed as incurable.*

The nature and circumstances of human illnesses that cause death have changed dramatically over the last century. No longer are tuberculosis, scarlet fever, and gastroenteritis diseases the major causes of death. These diseases, as well as most childhood illnesses, have been eliminated by medical science and modern health-care procedures. A comparison of the nine major causes of death in the United States uncovers the following rank order: (1) heart disease, (2) cancer, (3) strokes, (4) accidents, (5) influenza, pneumonia, (6) diabetes mellitus, (7) infants' diseases, (8) arteriosclerosis, (9) liver cirrhosis, and (10) bronchitis, emphysema, and asthma.

Thus, the communicable diseases of yesterday have been replaced by the degenerative diseases of today — cancer, heart attacks, and strokes. They are illnesses that primarily face our older population. A large number of younger persons are killed by diseases of pollution and those growing out of drug and alcohol abuse. The latter include bronchitis, emphysema, and cirrhosis. In addition to changes in diseases causing death, changes have also occurred in the age distribution of our population. Along with medical discoveries and improved medical procedures has come an increase in the number of years we can expect to live.

In 1900, 53 percent of all recorded deaths in the United States were children under the age of 15. The percentage of people dying over the age of 65 was only 17 percent. Today, the proportion of infants' deaths has declined from 150 to 25 out of every 1,000 live births. In the 1960s, the number of deaths of people over the age of 65 was 67 percent of all deaths. This was 1.5 million of the 2 million total deaths in the United States. It is predicted that the number of people over the age of 65 will increase from the 18.5 million who lived in the 1960s to 24.5 million by the late 1980s.[2] Currently, one-eighth of our total population are adults over the age of 65.

As our nation's life expectancy increases, so too does the number of people in the work force who have been diagnosed as chronically ill. In 1976, the number of terminally ill persons able to work, keep house, or engage in school activities was nearly 7.5 million. Another 15.2 million were able to participate in these activities to a limited degree. These numbers represent over 75 percent of those diagnosed as chronically ill. Also in 1976, it was estimated that the number totaled more than 8 million. Many of them are employed in human service agencies.[3]

A major concern of employers about the chronically ill is the number of absences they may have because of their illness. The statistics prove this fear to be exaggerated. Individuals with chronic illnesses generally have a lower percent of lost work days than those with acute illness (lasting less than three months).[4] Human service workers in particular tend to work "right up to the end." As Monroe Lerner said: "Whereas formerly people died on an average much earlier in life, victims primarily of communicable diseases, they survive today to a much later age, only to succumb in due time to the degenerative conditions."[5] These numbers then surely have an impact on our work force. More than ever before, working adults are now likely to become inflicted with terminal illnesses that lead to death.

Myths and Stereotypes

There is a popular, albeit false, belief that we cannot successfully prepare for death. Implicit in this view is the assumption that the process of dying is something that just happens and we have no control over it. This negates the human ability to make choices about how to live and, relatedly, how to die. Terminally ill workers can decide to live and die with dignity, or they can decide to grovel and whimper as life comes to an end. We need be no less ourselves in the stages of dying than we are in the preceding stages.

It is true that some people give up the struggle long before their vital life signs cease. This is not the kind of worker I am talking about. Rather, I am talking about terminally ill workers who:

1. *Are aware of their being.* They have the capacity to choose their own behavior.
2. *Assume responsibility for their behavior.* Life (and dying) is what they make it.

3. *Display the "courage to be."* They make decisions, assert themselves, and accept the consequences.

There are no rules of dying to show us how it ought to be done. This is a journey in which no regulations are warranted. Each person must interpret the meaning and the way of dying for himself or herself. Some writers state that it is hard to die. On the contrary, what is hard is living. It is absurd for people to ask whether there is an easy way to die — or live. Human existence means suffering; yet, suffering is positive and necessary for the progression of life. We are truly human when we accept the human condition: we exist, we work, we invent ourselves and assume responsibility for our lives, and we die. Living gives dying a meaning.

Another common myth is that it is better to shelter colleagues from our illnesses because sickness has no place on the job. We should, this line of reasoning continues, keep our personal problems to ourselves. Since humans are social creatures, in order to "be" sick they must disclose their illness to others, but this need not be an indiscriminant disclosure — it should be only to a few colleagues that we respect and like. It is only by sharing our frustrations, anxieties, and doubts that we are able to overcome these things. Just as we do not live alone, we need not be alone in death.

No doubt some of you will have heard the next myth: it is better not to talk about emotionally painful things with terminally ill workers. Balderdash! John Powell wrote: "Repressed emotions are the most common cause of fatigue and actual sickness. . . . Repressed emotions may find their outlet in the 'acting out' of headaches, skin rashes, allergies, asthma, common colds, tightened muscles, the slamming of doors, the clenching of fists, the rise of blood pressure, the grinding of teeth, tears, temper trantrums, acts of violence. We do not bury our emotions *dead*; they remain in our subconscious minds and intestines, to hurt and trouble us. It is not only much more conducive to a relationship to report our true feelings, but it is equally essential to our integrity and health."[6]

Unfortunately, most of the agency conversations involving terminally ill workers are at what John Powell called the fifth, fourth, and third levels. The outer, or fifth, level of communication is the "cliché conversation." At this level everyone is safe, for there is no sharing of personal feelings. The conversation is: "Hi. Hi. How are you? Fine, thank you. I'll be seeing you. So long." The ailing person senses the superficiality and obliges by giving socially correct answers.

The fourth level is the "reporting facts about others" level. During this type of interaction, we expose almost nothing of ourselves. We talk about what so-and-so has done or said. We seek refuge in gossip items and conversation pieces, giving nothing of ourselves and inviting nothing from others.

At the third level, called "my ideas and judgments," there is some risk taking in telling of ideas and decisions. However, we watch others closely and retreat to levels four or five if they show signs of disapproval. Even worse, we resort to saying things we do not mean because we sense they are what the other person wants to hear.

The second level is described as "my feelings and emotions." This is the "gut level," where we follow up the third-level statements with such things as "I don't know what to say to you." At this level there is mutual openness and honesty. Without this kind of communication, we cannot grow, nor can we help anyone else to grow.

The first level is the "peak communication" level. Peak communications are not permanent, but they are precious moments when the encounter with a terminally ill person attains almost perfect and mutual empathy. It is during this interaction that another myth about terminally ill persons is exploded: they are too preoccupied with their sickness and therefore cannot understand the sorrow or joys of others. The stereotype of terminally ill workers unable to rise above their anger or resignation in order to be an integral part of an agency team is, like most stereotypes, partially true. Some terminally ill workers fit this description, but most of them do not. In fact, most terminally ill workers give much to others and too little to themselves.

Those Who Are Affected

Agency workers tend to be more detached than their predecessors. Today's household consists of parents and children rather than three or four generations of relatives. Grandparents often live many miles away from their children. Indeed, grandchildren may only be aware of isolated communities or nursing homes where aging and dying occur out of the sights of the young. They tend to think of dying as happening to someone else. They generally do not experience death until they reach adulthood and deal with their grandparents' death. Perhaps Americans are, as Robert Fulton said, "The first death-free society."[7] People in our society are increasingly likely to be born, go through childhood, and enter adulthood before witnessing the natural death of a close relative or a friend.

Our loathing of death coupled with modern science and technology has given new reason to hope that with more advances in research and medicine we can do away with humanity's life-threatening illnesses. Although this may relieve our basic anxiety, it does nothing to dispel it. This feeling of discomfort about the topic of death is as common in the medical and allied health professions as it is in other professions. It is not reassuring to learn that physicians "are people with all the doubts, fears, uncertainties, and prejudices of people everywhere."[8] As a result of these fears, most physicians are conspicuously void of skills pertaining to counseling terminally ill people. Nor are most other helping professionals any better trained.

In 1970, *Psychology Today* attempted to break the conversation taboo surrounding dying by surveying its readers concerning their beliefs and attitudes about their death and dying. The questionnaire explored several aspects of dying. First, childhood experiences and attitudes were examined, including the earliest personal involvement with and family discussions of death. Other questions were directed at current beliefs and thoughts about one's own life as well as afterlife. The response to the questionnaire was overwhelming. More than 30,000 readers responded to the survey. Edwin Sneidman felt as though "thousands of persons had been waiting for a legitimate occasion to unburden themselves about death and then felt somehow cleansed after writing their unspoken thoughts."[9] A personality profile was derived from the survey. Sneidman wrote that the typical respondent is a 20-24 year old, single, Caucasian, (somewhat religious) Protestant, politically independent ("somewhat liberal") female. She is a college graduate, earns between $10,000 and $15,000 a year, lives in the Midwest, and comes from a small family (one sibling). She is in "very good" (but not "excellent") physical and mental health.[10]

The survey showed definite trends in the way the respondents viewed death. Considerable insight came from responses to the questions concerning childhood discussions of death within the family. One-third of the respondents could not recall from childhood any discussion of death. In 20 percent of the families the topic was discussed with discomfort, while 30 percent of the families discussed death openly. Nearly half of the respondents (43%) experienced death for the first time when their grandparents died. The majority became aware of death between the ages of five and ten, and their childhood conceptions of death were largely based on heaven-and-hell fantasies. By adulthood, the respondents' heaven-and-hell concepts had changed. The largest group (35%) viewed death as simply the final process of life. Only 29 percent believed in an afterlife, nearly half the number who believed in afterlife as a child.

A study by Hannelore Wass compared the views and opinions of an older population (65 years of age and older) with those in the *Psychology Today* study. His findings showed that the older group "differed significantly from Sneidman's young sample as expected—in that the elderly expressed more religious, conservative, and traditional views with respect to death, dying, and funeralization. At the same time, there were some striking similarities between the two groups, particularly in their concerns for survivors, their views on the timing of death, and on funeral practices."[11]

Unable to face the thought of no longer being, many human service workers comfort themselves with thoughts of a blissful, eternal afterlife. Social scientists and medical professionals are only beginning to explore the personal implications of death and dying. When these studies become commonplace, so too will the subject of death and dying. Until then, helping professionals are likely to engage in some very unhelpful behaviors when their colleagues cry out for assistance.

PSYCHOLOGY OF DYING. The psychological state of the terminally ill worker is perhaps the most important condition for us to understand. Empathizing with the shifting states of the ill worker is necessary for anyone in contact with him or her (i.e. the family, doctors, colleagues, and employers). Only recently has the psychology of dying been rigorously studied. The psychological factors are so important that they have been found to influence the timing of a worker's death.

Several programs have been established to secure data regarding the psychology of death. One of the most widely recognized research programs has been at the University of Chicago. It began under the direction of Elisabeth Kübler-Ross.[12] In this program an "instructor," who is actually a terminally ill patient, sits behind a one-way glass partition and talks to physicians, medical students, and nurses. The instructor voluntarily discusses his or her feelings, thoughts, hopes, and misgivings about life as death draws near. The seminars serve as therapy for the participants—patients as well as the observers. Since her initial studies, Kübler-Ross has talked with hundreds of dying patients. One of her most important contributions to the education of those concerned with helping terminally ill persons is her study of dying. Almost all terminally ill persons go through a series of predictable psychological states: denial and isolation, anger, bargaining, depression, and acceptance.[13]

The first reaction to the knowledge of terminal illness is usually to say, "No, the doctors have the wrong slide, the wrong x-ray. It can't be me." This is the denial phase. Denial is a general "term to cover any sort of behavior that allows a person to avoid facing reality, to evade confronting anything unpleasant."[14] It is a recognition of the reality followed by a rejection of the threatening aspects, replacing it with more comfortable reactions. The denial phase differs in each person in its intensity and its manifestation. The reaction may be momentary or for a lengthy period of time. Frequently, the stricken person will visit three or four different doctors for opinions and new tests. Even acceptance of the illness can involve denial. "One may accept the basic fact of being ill, but deny that one is seriously ill. One may accept that it is serious, but deny the diagnosis. One may accept the diagnosis, but deny that the condition is fatal. Even if one accepts that, one may deny that it bothers one at all or ignore its implications and consequences."[15]

Kübler-Ross cautions that we should be aware of the initial stage of a terminal illness. It "functions as a buffer after unexpected shocking news, allows the patient to collect himself and, with time, mobilize other, less radical defenses."[16] Denial is almost always a temporary defense which will be replaced with at least partial acknowledgment of the inevitable. The empathetic listener should be attuned to the worker's need to deny his or her impending death.

Anger is the feeling that often follows denial. The fantasy of being well until death is replaced with the reality of the illness. The reaction "No, it can't be me" gives way to the new feeling "Why me?" The worker begins to feel anger, rage, envy, and resentment or some combination of these feelings. A once controlled and polite person may suddenly lash out to those close by. The spouse does not know anything anymore, colleagues cannot be trusted, and members of the family just do not understand. The rage is directed at all people around the worker, especially close associates and loved ones. This stage is often the most difficult for colleagues to cope with. They usually receive little reciprocal warmness, which only makes job interactions more difficult. The worker's feelings of anger and hurt become a self-fulfilling prophecy as colleagues either respond with grief and tears, guilt, or shame or avoid the ill person, which only increases the worker's anger.

Then there comes a point when the worker realizes that anger is not the answer and he or she begins to bargain. This third stage is the most childish of the five phases. Kübler-Ross compared this stage with the all-too-familiar tactics of a child demanding favors and then asking for them. "They may not accept our 'No' when they want to spend a night in a friend's house. They may be angry and stamp their foot. They may lock themselves in their bedroom and temporarily express their anger by rejecting us. But they will also have second thoughts. They may consider another approach. They will eventually volunteer to do some tasks around the house, which under normal circumstances we never succeeded in getting them to do, and then tell us, 'if I am very good all week and wash the dishes every evening, then will you let me go?'"[17] Terminally ill workers use bargaining in much the same way. The promises to be better and more productive staff members are often made. This is an attempt to postpone the inevitable. It is a "phase of negotiating with reality, exploring to see if one can improve the terms and conditions of the contract."[18]

The fourth psychological stage the dying worker goes through is depression and sadness. This usually happens after many painful tests and symptoms which verify that the worker will never be the same again. The result of this realization may be feelings of depression—a reaction depression and a preparatory depression. Both are quite different and should be handled accordingly. The first type of depression is caused by a loss. There may be loss of job efficiency, financial security, house and possessions, and, more importantly, a loss of dreams. This type of depression is well known. The second type of depression, preparatory, manifests itself in sadness for the impending losses. The worker is in the process of losing all the activities, possessions, and people that he or she loves.

Members of the family and the helping profession should be aware of the functional role of depression. Often we will try to cheer terminally ill colleagues to get them to see the bright side of life. But this is usually an answer to our own needs rather than our dying colleagues'. In a state of depression, the ill worker can often be helped by colleagues by simply listening when he or she needs to talk and by being silent when he or she needs quiet inner reflection. Physical avoidance is not the answer.

Once the worker goes through the emotions of denying, anger, bargaining, and depression, the final phase—acceptance—begins. It is at this point that the worker is able to express feelings of envy, pain, and loss; only then is there a realistic expectation of the end. It is important, if possible, that the worker's colleagues be able to accept his or her death. An early resolution will allow time for all parties to work through lingering emotions to reach the stage of acceptance. An individual can be willing to die without being suicidal. Those around the worker should be aware of this so that they are able to let go at the appropriate time. It has been written that "a dying man needs time to die, as a sleepy man needs to sleep, and there comes a time when it is wrong, as well as useless, to resist."[19]

FAMILY CONCERNS. The most important support system for the terminally ill is the family. Family members play a significant role in the worker's response to the illness. We cannot help the terminally ill worker in the most meaningful way if we do not include his or her family.[20] Unfortunately, the family is often ignored. Just as the worker goes through a series of psychological stages, so too do members of his or her family. At first, they may deny that the illness is true, or they may try to shift the burden by seeking help from many sources and arranging trips to expensive physicians and medical centers. They may even deny to others that the worker is gravely ill.

The denial often turns to anger as members of the family begin to accept the illness. Again, there is anger at the physician, agency personnel, and friends for not caring enough no matter how hard they try. Of course, members of the family may be angry at themselves for not making the most of past opportunities to interact with the worker. Whatever the reasons, anger is normal.

After the anger wears away, the family faces preparatory grief. Often "relatives say proudly of themselves that they always tried to keep a smiling face when confronted with the patient, until one day they just could not keep the facade any longer."[21] In most cases this is just what the worker needs—true emotions spoken about the illness and his or her impending death. The earlier the family can reach this stage of discussing their true feeling toward the illness, the sooner they can reach a level of acceptance.

The illness may result in many changes in the family's day-to-day activities. When an adult is terminally ill, usually there is a spouse or some other loved one who is faced with continuing the responsibilities of her or his own role as well as the worker's. "Serious illness and hospitalization of a husband, for example, may bring about relevant changes in the household which the wife has to get accustomed to. She may feel threatened by the loss of security and the end of her dependence on her husband. She will have to take on many chores previously done by him and will have to adjust her own schedule to the new, strange, and increased demands. She may suddenly have to get involved in business matters and their financial affairs, which she previously avoided doing."[22]

Guilt is probably the hardest problem facing the worker's family. Often members of the family blame themselves for not noticing sooner, not taking better care of the sick person, not spending enough time with him or her, and so on. A neutral person may be needed to listen to the family members and to try to understand what they are feeling. It is not enough to respond to them by saying "No, it is not your fault. You did not cause the illness." The family needs to discuss their feelings and get to the reasons for their guilt. Frequently, individuals who work with the sick person can facilitate this dialogue.

PHYSICAL CONDITIONS. Pain is one of the greatest fears most people have of dying. In the *Psychology Today* survey discussed earlier, 15 percent of the respondents feared the pain of dying more than anything else associated with death.[23] Although it may be an inherent part of dying, pain is not necessarily an inevitable part. Because there are so many types of terminal illnesses, a simple conclusion cannot be drawn about the physical condition of the terminally ill. In general, a small number of individuals die suddenly and another small number have long periods of serious illness before they die. The majority of terminally ill persons require special care that may last for a few days or a week but not usually exceed three months.

It should also be acknowledged that it is often difficult to assess the amount of pain experienced by an individual. Physical distress is a vague symptom, subjective to each person, and very difficult to define or measure. If physicians and family members reacted to all aches due to discomfort, there would be (and probably is) an over-treatment of symptoms. Pain is not the only symptom that affects the physical condition of the dying. For example, nausea and vomiting often accompany kidney or liver diseases. Illness of the lungs or hearts often cause breathlessness, which may bring about a feeling of suffocation for the worker. The feeling of malaise or exhaustion is experienced by most people who have had long-term illnesses.

It seems that most of the physical distress of dying can be alleviated, but not all of it. The pain associated with cancer usually can be almost totally relieved. However, breathlessness remains an unsolved ailment of the dying process. In general, it can be said that unless the care is exceptional, about one-fifth of people dying in hospitals are apt to endure physical discomfort for an appreciable amount of time. Colleagues visiting them should try to not be unnerved by this condition. Of course, this is much easier said than done.

Special Programs

Earlier, we examined current views of dying and death. No social agency is free from workers who get ill and die. Therefore, in order to be optimally effective in helping terminally ill workers, there must be a willingness on the part of the helping professions to learn how to responsibly and carefully help the terminally ill. The foremost question to be answered is: How can we prepare helping professionals to meet the needs of the terminally ill? Ernest Morgan directly addressed the issue: "Why death education? Death education relates not only to death itself but to our feelings about ourselves and nature and the universe we live in. It has to do with our values and ideals, the way we relate to one another and the kind of world we are building. Thoughtfully pursued, it can deepen the quality of our lives and of our relationships."[24]

Once the importance of death education is recognized, the question of what should be taught must be answered. Three broad topics are recommended: (1) emphasis on death as a *personal* phenomenon, (2) examination of the *sociocultural* dimensions of death, and (3) a study of the *economic* aspects of death and dying.

These three areas seem crucial for any death-education program. The personal as well as professional dimensions of the problem will not allow helpers to think of dying and something "out there." There should be a mixture of personal values clarification, a look at societal values, and information about the financial aspects of dying. All of these impact on treatment. Basic to the entire process is sorting out one's own feelings about dying and death. The primary purpose of death education should focus on helping each of us get in touch with what best facilitates a minimum-stress ending to a life.

Agency directors concerned about their terminally ill employees should begin on-the-job education programs for them and their colleagues. Psychological and technical counseling as well as

job changes are usually needed. These programs should not penalize participants in terms of income or sick benefits. Employees
who are terminally ill should have opportunity to receive paid psychological counseling in or outside the agency. A general rule of
thumb is to go outside the agency for this service. An impartial,
trained professional can be a key in helping the worker and his or
her colleagues clarify their thoughts and feelings about dying.
Both the agency and employees will benefit from having this type
of assistance. Sandra Galdier Wilcox and Marilyn Sutton outlined
goals for such a counseling program:

1. Sharing the responsibility for the crisis of dying with the patient
   so that he has help in dealing with the first impact of anxiety and
   bewilderment.
2. Clarifying and defining the realities of the day-to-day existence
   that can be dealt with by the patient. These are the realities of his
   life.
3. Making continued human contact available and rewarding.
4. Assisting in the separation from and grief over the realistic losses
   of family, body image, and self-control, while retaining communication and meaningful relationships with those who will be lost.
5. Assuming necessary body and ego functions for the person without incurring shame or depreciation, maintaining respect for the
   person, and helping him maintain his self-respect.
6. Encouraging the person to work out an acceptance of his life situation with dignity and integrity so that gradual regression may
   occur without conflict or guilt.[25]

Terminally ill workers face many barriers in their work environments. Current laws do not cover their needs. Ironically,
many organizations in an effort to be fair to employees inadvertently, or in some cases purposely, create barriers for the terminally ill. Almost all compensation policies base benefits (e.g. pensions, health and life insurance, sick leave, and other benefits) on
seniority. These conditions negatively affect young, ill workers,
who often are not given a chance to earn these important benefits.

In many agencies, workers who have been diagnosed as terminally ill are bypassed for promotions. A large number of terminally ill workers are able to give many more years of valuable service
to an organization than their employers allow them. Helping agencies and other organizations treat the terminally ill as if they are
dead before they have quit living. Michael Simpson found that

"nearly a quarter of a group studied by an American Cancer Society team had been rejected for jobs because of their cancer treatment; nearly a quarter said they had met discrimination at work; about a fifth felt that their working conditions or salary had been adversely affected. Relations with fellow workers were strained. Some people thought that cancer was contagious and avoided the patients. Others were intrusive and gossipy or overprotective."[26]

The Rehabilitation Act of 1973 was intended to cover the terminally ill, but its scope is too broad. The act (1) requires government contractors to undertake an affirmative action program to hire the handicapped and (2) prohibits discrimination on the part of the contractors against the handicapped as long as they are qualified to do the work. In reality, this act has had very little effect on the treatment of the terminally ill. The vagueness and indirect relationship of the act to the terminally ill has resulted in employers almost totally misusing fatally ill workers.

An encouraging act was the passage of legislation in California directly dealing with the terminally ill. In 1975, a bill was passed that made illegal job discrimination because of a medical condition. However, the definition of "a medical condition" was extremely limited: "any health impairment related to or associated with a diagnosis of cancer, from which a person has been rehabilitated or cured."

Agency personnel with fatal illnesses are often faced with many legal and technical details concerning their impending deaths: funeral or cremation planning, writing a will, financial planning, and decisions about body or organ donation. Expert counseling in these areas is important and expensive. Agencies could help their workers by underwriting these services. Another need of terminally ill workers is job change or restructuring their responsibilities. For example, a job-sharing program could be established. In such a program, two employees share a single job. Usually, one employee works the first half of the day and a second works the latter, or flexible time schedules are implemented. Equal responsibility is given to both employees.

Job sharing can benefit ailing workers. It would ease them into fewer work hours. This, then, is a way for gradually phasing the employee into a reduced work schedule and, finally, retirement or termination. Each worker should have the option of remaining on the job without being forced to resign or retire as long as he or she is able to work. As aspects of helpers' jobs become computerized, terminally ill employees may soon have the opportunity to do a portion of their work from a terminal installed in their homes. The workers would key-in data to a computer. The comfort of home and the latitude of deciding when to work may greatly benefit fatally ill workers. Thus, many employees will be able to remain productive after being homebound.

In summary, too many social agencies treat death and dying as Thomas's *Do Not Go Gentle Into That Good Night.* Dying is still something evil that should be feared and avoided. We do not comfortably talk about dying, as if by ignoring it, it will go away. Fortunately, each year more helping professionals are getting involved in research, readings, and workshops focusing on dying and death. The terminally ill worker is gradually being seen as he or she is: a human being with feelings and emotions rather than merely a biological organism wasting away into nothingness.

Techniques and Tips

This is an appropriate place to pull together some of the themes found in dealing with other human resource problems. Throughout the previous sections, I have focused on a "be-it-yourself" approach. To be aware and to care about the world, values, and problems of one's colleagues is a significant aspect of the helping relationship. Perhaps when working with the terminally ill we are given our most difficult challenge. It is then that we come face-to-face with an individual's need for three areas of growth: inclusion, control, and affection.

> *Inclusion* refers to the need to be with people and to be alone. The effort in inclusion is to have enough contact to avoid loneliness and enjoy people; enough aloneness to avoid enmeshment and enjoy solitude. The fully realized man can feel comfortable and joyful both with and without people, and knows with how much of each, and when, he functions best.
>
> In the area of *control*, the effort is to achieve enough influence so that a man can determine his future to the degree that he finds most comfortable and to relinquish enough so that he is able to lean

on others, to teach, guide, support, and at times to take some responsibility from him. The fully realized man is capable of either
leading or following as appropriate and knowing where he personally
feels most comfortable.

   In *affection* the effort is to avoid being engulfed in emotional
entanglement. . . , but also to avoid having too little affection and a
bleak, sterile life without love, warmth, tenderness, and someone to
confide in.[27]

Colleagues of a terminally ill worker frequently behave like
members of his or her family. That is, they frequently take over,
try to rescue, and solve problems for the ill worker; and, like family members, they are unaware that a worker's life may depend on
him or her selecting and using indigenous resources.[28] When helpers behave in this manner, it is usually based on their need to be
supportive and caring. It is neither wise nor helpful to try to rescue people. It is better to *ask* how we may be of assistance. Too
often, helpers assume that their critically ill colleagues need protecting and to be dependent on others. Again, that may only be
our need, not our terminally ill colleagues'. There are several
things we can do in preparation for working with a terminally ill
colleague, including the following:

1. Discuss how we view the worker's contribution to the team
   effort.
2. Examine our own feelings about the worker's illness.
3. Look for ways to fulfill the worker's needs.
4. Ask ourselves and the ill worker how we can all best handle
   the illness.

There are no easy answers or foolproof tips on how to gracefully and inoffensively die with a colleague. There is no painless
way to prepare ourselves for the inevitable. The answer (if there is
one) must come from the way in which we *live* with our colleagues.
The plaudits, the questions, the apologies, the confessions, the rep-
rimands, the anger, and the joy are best done before the funeral.
In short, we should finish as much of the business of living as possible.

There is nothing new in this section for individuals who have
been well trained in the process of death counseling. There may,
however, be encouragement for renewed commitment to do a

better job as a professional helper as the day-to-day stress takes its toll in human service agencies. Austin Kutscher put this in proper perspective: "Man cannot face the sun, but he must nevertheless face his own death if he is to live. He must accept death as a part of life—as a prerequisite for his enjoyment of and formal acceptance of the full beauty and tragedy of life. Just as it is possible for the dying person to achieve acceptance of his own death and die in dignity, so too the living who are bereaved can, with help, be brought to accept a life in which death is an integral part. The challenge to us all is at least twofold: where is our place in the continuum at any time? How can we be effective as clinicians, as scientists and as human beings?"[29]

REFERENCES

1. Thomas, D.: "Do Not Go Gentle Into That Good Night." In *Poems of Dylan Thomas*. New York: New Directions, 1952, p. 25.
2. Sneidman, E.S. (Ed.): *Death: Current Perspectives*. Palo Alto, CA: Mayfield, 1976, p. 58.
3. National Center for Health Statistics: *Health Interview Survey*. Washington, D.C.: U.S. Government Printing Office, 1976, p. 14.
4. Ibid.
5. Lerner, M.: When, why, and where people die. In O.G. Brim, H. Freeman, S. Levine, and N. Scotch (Eds.): *The Dying Patient*. New York: Russell Sage Foundation, 1970, p. 10.
6. Powell, J.: *Why Am I Afraid to Tell You Who I Am?* Chicago: Argus Communications, 1969, p. 75.
7. Fulton, R.: *Death and Identity*, rev. ed. Bowie, MD: Charles Press, 1976, p. 8.
8. DeVrie, A., and Cari, A.: *The Dying Humans*. Ramet Gan, Israel: Turtledove, 1979, p. 26.
9. Sneidman, E.S.: You and Death. *Psychology Today, 5:*43, 1971.
10. Ibid.
11. Wass, H.: *Dying: Facing the Facts*. New York: McGraw-Hill, 1979, p. 71.
12. Kübler-Ross, E. (Ed.): *Death: The Final Stage of Growth*. Englewood Cliffs, NJ: Prentice-Hall, 1975.
13. Imara, M.: Dying as the last stage of growth. In Kübler-Ross, Ibid., p. 161.
14. Simpson, M.A.: *The Facts of Death*, Englewood Cliffs, NJ: Prentice-Hall, 1979, p. 37.
15. Ibid., p. 36.
16. Kübler-Ross, E.: *On Death and Dying*. New York: Macmillan, 1969.

17. Ibid., p. 82.
18. Simpson, *The Facts of Death*, p. 42.
19. Ibid., p. 43.
20. Kübler-Ross, *On Death and Dying*, p. 157.;
21. Ibid., p. 169.
22. Ibid., p. 157.
23. Sneidman, You and Death, p. 76.;
24. Morgan, E.: *A Manual of Death Education and Simple Burial.* Burnsville, NC: Celo Press, 1977, p. 3.
25. Wilcox, S.G. and Sutton, M.: *Understanding Death and Dying: An Interdisciplanary Approach.* Dominquez Hills, CA: California State College, 1977, p. 97.
26. Simpson, M.: *The Facts of Death*, p. 113.
27. Schutz, W.C.: *Joy: Expanding Human Awareness.* New York: Grove Press, 1967, p. 19.
28. Simonton, C.O., Matthews-Simonton, S., and Creighton, J.: *Getting Well Again.* Los Angeles: J.P. Tarcher, 1978.
29. Kutscher, A.H.: Anticipatory grief, death and bereavement: A continuum. In G. Henderson, (Ed.): *Physician-Patient Communication,* Springfield, IL: Charles C Thomas, Publisher, 1981, p. 163.

Chapter 9
EFFECTIVE HELPERS

IT is prudent for professional helpers not to delude themselves into believing that they are free of prejudices and, consequently, treat all people the same. *Helpers do have favorites.* In fact, we all are prejudiced for or against someone or something. To say that we are not will render us unable to compensate for these feelings. It is human for helpers to have preferences. Some human service workers are uncomfortable around ethnic minorities; others prefer not to work with women or older persons. Still others have little respect or no use for recovered alcoholics and other previously ill persons. Few helpers are comfortable with the terminally ill.

Seldom are we neutral in our feelings about people with whom we work. Moreover, we tend to be conscious of the prejudices of others but not our own. Being culturally conditioned, our attitudes, feelings, and values make objective thinking difficult. Not even college classes and on-the-job experiences can completely eradicate earlier conditioning. For this reason, it is both behaviors and beliefs that comprise the major problems in the helping process. Because most helpers define themselves as being well adjusted, they frequently are shocked, outraged, frightened, or even hostile when they encounter maladjusted colleagues who ask for help.

Prejudiced Helpers

Few helpers are adequately trained to assist colleagues (whatever their relationship) resolve personal problems. Many professionals believe that docility, punctuality, and unquestioned obedience are the hallmarks of a good worker. Individuals who deviate from organization norms are labeled "weird" or "queer" or "over the hill." The most insidious aspect of labeling colleagues is associating them with the salvageable people our society all too readily throws away. In previous chapters, I have described some of the personnel we throw away.

The more effective helpers are able to manage their negative feelings. This is not to imply that they are completely objective and treat all colleagues equally, but that they minimize unfair treatment and maximize fair treatment. Getting to know other people may not alter our negative attitudes toward their behavior, but we will be better able to respond therapeutically to them. While it could be ideal, a helper need not like a colleague in order to help him or her. Understanding and empathy can occur without condemning or liking the individual.

There are no truly homogeneous groups of helpers. Within each organization there are noticeable differences in life-styles, aspirations, education, and abilities. Having a professional degree or title is not per se an absolute determinant of competence. Nor do differences in age, gender, color, ethnic background, or health automatically result in professional skills or deficiencies. We have to learn to be good helpers and this is hard, demanding work. Part of the education for effectiveness is learning the lesson that similarity in skin color, age, ethnic background, and gender do not mean sameness in every respect. In unguarded moments of conversation, our prejudices peek through. According to Carl Jung:

> In daily life it happens all the time that we presume that the psychology of other people is the same as ours. We suppose that what is pleasing or desirable to us is the same to others and that what seems bad to us must also seem bad to them. It is only recently that our courts of law have nerved themselves to admit the psychological relativity of guilt in pronouncing sentence. . . . And we still attribute to the other fellow all the evil and inferior qualities that we do not like to recognize in ourselves, and therefore have to criticize and attack him, when all that has happened is that an inferior 'soul' has emigrated from one person to another. The world is still full of bêtes noires and scapegoats, just as it formerly teemed with witches and werewolves.[1]

Helping is complicated by the fact that each helper is a complex personality. A helper's psychological needs, values, and prejudices determine his or her approach to clients and colleagues. Despite a certain amount of variability, both helpers and helpees develop fairly stable, stereotyped ways of dealing with each other. Some human service personnel are oversensitive and see insult where none was intended. Long before entering their professions, some of these workers have become cynical and disillusioned about themselves, their chosen professions, and life in general. Others get this way after being subjected to failures on the job. Thus, they come to work bitter, hostile, and rebellious. For example, some minority workers become supersensitive to racial slurs, women to sexist behavior, and older workers to ageism.

Supervisors determined to "show their people who's the boss" are likely to discover how obstinate and recalcitrant their subordinates can be. A helper's behavior should say to colleagues, "I am here to understand you so that I can help you." This type of authority extends beyond keeping order and monitoring the work flow. Respect for authority should not be confused with fear. Ailing and discriminated workers, more so than others, need to feel that their colleagues and supervisors understand and accept them as individuals of unique value.

Workers who have not been accepted by their peers and made to feel wanted will find it extremely difficult to relate to their supervisors and peers in a positive manner. They may withdraw, not pay attention in staff meetings, complain easily, or become discipline problems. It is important to note that many rejected workers appear to have no motivation, no aspirations, and no interest in their careers. These workers are not mentally retarded, rather, they are rejecting their rejectors. They have no desire or interest in being hurt again.

Helpers must be able to give of themselves and to receive from their helpees. The act of unconditional acceptance communicates to colleagues, "I acknowledge your existence, but I will not cause you to lose your identity." Acceptance does not mean feeling *like* others but feeling *with* them. No individual can ever feel like another because no two persons live in the same cognitive world. The behavior of each worker is not determined solely by the organization environment but also by the environment outside the agency. By trying, white workers frequently can understand the effects of minority status, males can understand female status, young workers can understand the psychological disposition of older workers, and well workers can understand sick ones. Prejudice is not an innocuous children's game. Contrary to popular notion, words can hurt—they can set in motion behaviors that socially, psychologically, and economically cripple people.

An optimum helper–helpee relationship involves two people freely responding to each other. This does not mean that the relationship will always be pleasant. Rather, it is an encounter in which both parties feel free to say "I agree" or "I disagree." There are many reasons an open, honest interaction with their colleagues can be beneficial to wasted workers in their search for identity and happiness. From the other side, there are some obvious risks in caring about colleagues who are "different." They are promoted or fired, rehabilitated or get worse. In some communities, they continually move from one job to another.

The temporary nature of most helper–helpee relationships can be heartbreaking for both the helper and the helpee. This is compounded by the fact that some helpers develop negative concepts of themselves or work habits that no colleague can assist them to alter. To care under this condition is to become frustrated by the inability to succeed. Some workers are afraid to care because they are afraid that they will lose newly achieved status. Upwardly mobile black workers, for example, who identify with whiteness are sometimes unwilling to help other minorities. These black Anglo-Saxons are determined to prove that they are better than other minorities. Their self-hatred is intensified when community norms force them to live in minority neighborhoods. But this is not unique to minorities. Some women reject other women, alcoholics reject alcoholics, older workers reject older workers, et cetera.

Because a major aspect of most helpers' behavior is the result of their self-concepts and how their colleagues view them, we should not be surprised when rejected workers act out their low self-image. In some instances, culturally, physically, or mentally different workers will test their colleagues to see if they will turn against them. They will ask coworkers to give more of themselves than is humanly possible, thereby trying to justify their own negative acts. Throughout these trials, helpers should try not to be hostile to colleagues whose behavior is irritating, attacking, or demanding. Helpers who respond by attacking, degrading, or destroying a colleague's self-esteem are not being professionally or personally helpful. Upon close examination, many hostile colleagues who need help are actually performing much better than their conditions would suggest.

Records and Reputation

Every worker has an academic record, an employment record, and a social reputation, all of which precede and follow him or her. Academic records mainly consist of college grades, while employment records chronicle the jobs and positions one has held. Social reputations are an imprecise mixture of anecdotal records and rumors. Seldom do records or reputations acknowledge unequal opportunities, myths and stereotypes, and other circumstances beyond the control of the worker. If taken at face value, some administrators will be horrified or ecstatic at the mere thought of hiring certain individuals.

The workers described in this book are frequently handicapped by their administrators' and colleagues' low expectations of them. Despite thousands of volumes detailing environmental blockages faced by certain kinds of workers, most administrators continue to look mainly at accomplishments instead of potentials. Far too many professional helpers cling to the myth that some individuals (e.g. alcoholics, terminally ill, and older workers) are not salvageable. There is a strong temptation to accept an individual's records or reputation as gospel. By so doing, we are relieved of the tiresome burden of individualizing our behavior for people we think we do not like or cannot salvage. To quote Carl Jung:

> There is and can be no self-knowledge based on theoretical assumptions, for the object of self-knowledge is an individual — a relative expectation and an irregular phenomenon. Hence it is not the universal and the regular that characterize the individual, but rather the unique. He is not to be understood as a recurrent unit but as something unique and singular. . . . At the same time man, as member of a species, can and must be be described as a statistical unit; otherwise

nothing general could be said about him. . . . The individual, however, as an irrational datum, is the true and authentic carrier of reality, the *concrete* man as opposed to the unreal ideal or normal man
to whom the scientific statements refer.[2]

It is of utmost importance that those involved in the helping
relationship always keep in mind the injunction to avoid labeling,
stereotyping, generalizing, categorizing, and rationalizing the
unique human being who defies the reduction and simplification
provided by his or her records and reputation. Quantified data certainly have their place and can provide us with varied and invalua-
ble heuristic tools to use in our roles as helpers, but we must be
willing and prepared to discard these tools when they do not fit or
when they cease to lend understanding of the individual with
whom we are helping.

The best way to learn what our colleagues are like is to observe
their behavior, listen to their conversation, and let them tell us
about themselves. It is a rare experience for a helper to talk with
coworkers who, instead of criticizing, listen without judging. It is
even rarer for workers in trouble to talk with coworkers who do
not admonish them but listen in an effort to better understand
and help them. The major difference between an effective helper
and an ineffective one is that the former listens with a sensitive ear
and the latter with a deaf ear. When a colleague asks for help, he
or she usually needs to be assured of being understood and respected.

BEING UNDERSTOOD. It seems easier for helpers to apply
basic principles of helping with strangers than with colleagues and
friends. For example, civil rights organizations tend to have racist
and sexist behaviors unchecked, chemical dependency agencies
work more effectively with alcoholic clients than with alcoholic
colleagues, and mental institutions diagnose and rehabilitate clients who walk in from the street but seem impotent to abate the
maladjustment among their own staffs. It is not that most helpers
do not know what to do; they just do not know what to do for
themselves and their colleagues.

When helpers are sick or need assistance, they want their colleagues to show friendly, warm interest. They want to be seen as
persons. They do not want to be analyzed and intellectualized.

The helping encounter is most effective between *people* rather than between *concepts* and *theories*. They want to be able to tell their story in their own way and in their own time. Equally important, they want to be heard. True, they may ramble, digress, seem to be incoherent, and at times bring in extraneous details, but they want to tell it. They do not want their colleagues to put words in their mouths or try to make the hurt disappear. In short, they want the best treatment a professional helper has been taught to provide.

Distressed workers are helped to tell their stories by thoughtful questions. Rules of thumb for asking questions are: (1) determine what is needed to understand the problem; (2) ask questions that show the other person we are interested in him or her; (3) if a question can wait for another time, don't ask it; and (4) ask only questions necessary in offering the help that is needed. Carefully worded and timely questions can let a colleague know that his or her situation is appreciated.

Colleagues seeking help should not be judged as good or bad persons. Whatever their situation, if we agree to help, we should suspend value judgments. If our values are unalterably in conflict with a colleague's behavior or condition, then we should refer him or her to someone else. Useful help is not likely to come from helpers with hang-ups about the helpee's condition. For example, a white racist should not counsel a minority worker complaining about job discrimination. Self-knowledge is an important characteristic of a helper. According to Maurice Nicoll:

> No one as he is mechanically — that is, as formed by life and its influences — can enter into and understand another, and, from that, give help, unless he already knows from his own self-observation, self-study and insight and work on himself, what is in the other person. Only through self-knowledge is knowledge of others practically possible. . . . One of the greatest evils of human relationships is that people make no attempt to enter into another's position but merely criticize one another without any restraint and do not possess any inner check to this mechanical criticism owing to the absence of any insight into themselves and their own glaring crudities, faults and shortcomings.[3]

Beyond the noble injunctions to be nonjudgmental and empathic, there are several reasons it is difficult to behave in this way:

1. The actions of colleagues frequently make it difficult to be understanding.
2. It is seldom easy or natural for most of us to be understanding persons.
3. There are times when everyone in an organization is offended by the behavior of a colleague.

These factors reinforce the need for self-awareness. The more we know and understand our own values, prejudices, and aspirations, the better able we are to cope with our colleague's problems in a therapeutic manner.

BEING RESPECTED. According to Carl Rogers, the helping relationship is a professional challenge: "To be faced by a troubled conflicted person who is seeking and expecting help has always constituted a great challenge to me. Do I have the knowledge, the resources, the psychological strength, the strength—do I have whatever it takes to be of help to such an individual?"[4] Central to the helping process is respect for the helpee.

Thus, a helping relationship can become the focal point for experiencing the world as a totality through recognition of the other. But we may find even more than this through what Martin Buber called the *I—Thou relationship:* "Creatures are placed in my way so that I, and the fellow creatures, by means of them and with them find the ways to God."[5] The opposite of the loving, revealing I—Thou relationship is the I—It relationship, which is dehumanizing and destructive. Colleagues whom we do not like become Its—they are treated as objects rather than subjects. According to Anthony Storr:

> To incorporate another person is to swallow him up, to overwhelm him, and to destroy him; and thus to treat him ultimately as less than a whole person. To identify with another person is to lose oneself, to submerge one's own identity in that of the other, to be overwhelmed, and hence to treat oneself ultimately as less than a whole person. To pass judgment, in Jung's sense, is to place oneself in an attitude of superiority; to agree offhandedly is to place oneself in an attitude of inferiority. . . . The personality can cease to exist in two ways—either by destroying the other, or being absorbed by the other—and maturity in interpersonal relationships demands that neither oneself nor the other shall disappear, but that each shall contribute to the affirmation and realization of the other's personality.[6]

It is not uncommon for workers to maintain anxieties that are not easily pinpointed. Such workers are plagued with pervasive apprehensions of impending disasters. Sometimes the mere thought of going to work is enough to produce physiological states of anxiety—rapid heartbeat, upset stomach, sweating, and trembling. Fear is one of the most troublesome of all emotional reactions. From the point of view of the workers experiencing it, fear disables them at a time they most need to remain calm. Often, the source of fear is unknown, has been forgotten or repressed. It is difficult to respect colleagues who succumb to fears that we push aside.

Anxiety is an irrational fear not directed at an appropriate target and not controlled by objective insight. Anxiety, then, is a vague expectation of danger. Gordon Allport compared it with a grease spot that spreads throughout life and stains the individual's professional and social relationships.[7] Most human service personnel tend to be ashamed of anxiety, since their ethical codes place a high premium on courage and self-reliance. The worker who lives in constant fear of failing imagines that he or she is surrounded by potentially dangerous forces, such as defective equipment, hostile coworkers, and non-supportive supervisors. Some anxieties develop into phobias. As James E. Gordon states: "Phobias are usually experienced as strong apprehension and anxiety when in the presence of the phobic object or situation, a fear that can develop into panic proportions in which the person blindly flees in a loss of self-control from the phobic situation. . . . The phobic person usually takes steps to avoid the phobic situation, and these steps often produce a restriction on his life which makes it more difficult for him to engage in the usual social interactions."[8]

Most workers want their colleagues to think highly of them and they, in turn, want to think highly of their colleagues. The performance of either feat is improbable if the worker is not aware of his or her fears or those of his or her colleagues. Initially, the help that an individual seeks is help in overcoming fears of failure.

Problem Solving

The dynamics of problem solving in human relations are three-fold:

1. The facts that constitute the problem must be understood. Facts frequently consist of both objective reality and subjective reactions.
2. The facts must be thought through. They must be probed into, reorganized, and turned over in order for the distressed worker to grasp as much of the total configuration as possible.
3. A decision must be made that will result in resolving or alleviating the problem. This usually involves a change in behavior and, if possible, attitude.

Succinctly, the three operations of problem solving are fact-finding, analysis of facts, and implementation of conclusions. For greatest effectiveness, workers must be fully involved in the efforts to solve their problems. It is possible for a colleague to define the problem and prescribe solutions, but when this happens the worker's self-responsibility is weakened. It is always better if the individuals who have the problem are able to bring about the resolution.

A problem cannot be solved if necessary information is missing. A helper may want to understand his or her colleagues but be unable to do so because some of the data is missing or distorted. Sometimes a colleague may not be privy to all the information. In other instances, the information may have been misinterpreted. Like any puzzle, missing pieces of information in a human relations problem will render it insolvable. Briefly, I will discuss other aspects of problem solving.

INFORMATION ALONE IS SELDOM ENOUGH. Too much information can freeze negative attitudes and reinforce dysfunctional behavior. Conditioned by parental and peer group norms, contradictory information may only cause the worker to say, "I understand what you have said, but I don't believe it." For example, a sexist male may disregard scientific studies documenting female abilities to do male-oriented jobs. An individual with delusions of grandeur is not likely to believe reports documenting his mediocrity. Thus, in order to be helpful, information must be believed by the worker.

SENSITIVITY IS THE CAPACITY TO IDENTIFY AND EMPATHIZE WITH THE VALUES, ASPIRATIONS, AND FEELINGS

OF OUR COLLEAGUES. Today, more than ever, we need sensitive helpers. Without being able to see others as they see themselves, to dispel fears of cultural differences, and to communicate with their colleagues, helpers will turn their organizations into socially and psychologically destructive battlefields. If helpers are unable to put themselves in the minds of their colleagues, there will be little help for the ailing persons. To quote Karl Menninger: "When a trout rising to a fly gets hooked on a line and finds himself unable to swim about freely, he begins with a fight which results in struggles and splashes and sometimes an escape. Often, of course, the situation is too tough for him. Sometimes he masters his difficulties; sometimes they are too much for him. His struggles are all that the world sees and it naturally misunderstands them. It is hard for a free fish to understand what is happening to a hooked one."[9] It is precisely this understanding that forms the *raison d'être* of the helping relationship—that is, for a psychologically mature human being to counsel, care for, or administer therapy to another human being in conflict or feeling uncomfortable with himself or herself, other persons, the environment, or any combination of these.

FREQUENTLY, HELPERS ARE PROBLEMS THEMSELVES OR CAUSES OF PROBLEMS. As noted earlier, the ability of helpers to achieve and maintain a condition of objectivity when dealing with their colleagues' problems is important in the helping process. If the helper gets wrapped up in his or her own inner world, he or she will not be able to perceive clearly the feelings of others. The challenge to helpers is awesome: they must feel but not to the point of losing their objectivity. Control of one's own feelings requires putting aside feelings that may be vital fibers of one's personality.

THE HELPER MUST CONSCIOUSLY FOCUS ON FEELINGS. Even when colleagues resist these efforts, the helper must do so in such a way as to communicate, "If you do not understand or agree with my perceptions, I will not reject you." Facts alone are relatively ineffective in altering deep-seated stress. Besides, facts include accounts and events seen and felt by the distressed worker. For this reason, workers must be allowed and, if necessary, encouraged to express their feelings so that the helper is focusing on the same issues.

IN MANY INSTANCES, AILING OR AGGRIEVED WORK-
ERS DO NOT KNOW HOW THEY REALLY FEEL ABOUT
THEIR SITUATION UNTIL THEY HAVE COMMUNICATED
THESE FEELINGS TO SOMEONE ELSE. Distressed workers may
only be aware of internal discomforts. Providing opportunities for
them to tell how they feel is usually the first step in isolating negative feeling and related behaviors. They may have previously communicated internal discomforts by arguing with, laughing at, or
avoiding contact with other workers. Talking about negative feelings can provide a better view of them and, hopefully, a better
chance for managing them. While allowing a colleague to "tell" is
a valuable technique in resolving problems, it is only a first step.
Telling should be related to some end and not merely an end in itself. *Solutions must be sought*. To quote William Glasser:

> In their unsuccessful effort to fulfill their needs, no matter what be-
> havior they chose, all [distressed workers] have a common charac-
> teristic: They deny the reality of the world around them. Some
> break the law, denying the rules of society; some claim their neigh-
> bors are plotting against them, denying the improbability of such be-
> havior. Some are afraid of crowded places, close quarters, airplanes,
> or elevators, yet they freely admit the irrationality of their fears.
> Millions drink to blot out the inadequacy they feel but that need not
> exist if they could learn to be different. . . . Therapy will be success-
> ful when they are able to give up denying the world and to recognize
> that reality not only exists but that they must fulfill their needs
> within its framework.[10]

Perhaps the major distinction lies between *talking about* a
problem and *talking through* it. In the first instance, usually nothing more than random talk, free association of ideas occurs. In the
second instance, more structured thinking occurs: a problem is
acknowledged, its implications and related behaviors examined,
and solutions pondered. Talking through a problem excites all the
body processes, often causing increased heartbeat and sweating.
The whole person gets caught up in it.

IT IS IMPERATIVE THAT DISTRESSED WORKERS FOCUS
ON PROBLEMS THAT CAN BE SOLVED. This is by far the most
efficient use of one's energies. For example, an older worker focusing on his age, a woman on her gender, or a terminal patient on
his illness are all wasting valuable time and energy, as they cannot

alter these things. However, if they focused on ageism, sexism, or ways of spending their remaining time, then something constructive is possible. Helpers must also focus on problems that have the potential of being solved. Some of the questions to be answered by the helpee during this process are:

- What is the problem? (Who did what, when, where, what happened?)
- Who senses (feels) the problem? (Only you, coworkers, supervisors?)
- How are you personally affected? (Emotionally, socially, economically, professionally?)
- What was the immediate cause for what happened?
- What organization rules and regulations pertain to the problem?
- Who can act to resolve this problem?
- What do you want to happen?
- What are your options?
- What will you do?

Whether we are involved in a helping relationship as professionals or as friends and confidants, it is inevitable that at some point in the relationship the issue of making choices will arise. The right kind of choosing is essential to bringing about a change in an individual or an organization. Helping relationships in which choosing is continually delayed or postponed by the helper and avoided by the worker are not helpful.

Rollo May sees the choosing of values as the central concern and goal toward which a person must move if he or she is to grow and eventually become integrated as a human being. "The Human Being not only *can* make such choices of values and goals," May wrote, "but he is the animal who *must* do so if he is to attain integration. For the value—the goal he moves toward—serves him as a psychological center, a kind of core of integration which draws together his powers as the core of a magnet draws the magnet's lines of force together."[11] Knowing what one feels and what one wants are the foundation blocks of change. The mark of mature persons is that their living is integrated into self-chosen goals. Someone must help ailing and aggrieved human service workers to choose and achieve healthy goals.

In Retrospect

A major problem in the helping professions is delusions and phobias. The *maladjusted professional worker delusion* and the *maladjusted professional worker phobia* may be the most pervasive factors causing and perpetuating inadequate care for human service professionals. As noted earlier, a delusion is a false judgment, while a phobia is an unreasonable and persistent fear of some object or situation and an attempt to avoid it. Both words are used by psychologists to indicate disorders in the cognitive processes of individuals. However, I use the terms to designate sociopsychological disorders that affect not only individuals but also groups. In addition, unlike psychological usages, I use the terms to imply highly contagious social conditions transmitted culturally through the process of socialization.

Thus, the maladjusted professional worker delusion is a false belief that workers who deviate from the norm because of gender, ethnic identity, age, or other conditions cited in this book are professionally inferior. The maladjusted professional worker phobia is an unsubstantiated and persistent fear of workers who deviate from the norm, and an effort is made to avoid contact with them. The viable options for maladjusted workers are as follows: (1) change their jobs, (2) change their attitudes and behaviors, (3) change their colleagues' attitudes and behaviors, and (4) do nothing. Of course, some combination of the first three options are possible.

Extremely neurotic or psychotic workers foster aspirations that have little or no relation to reality. Excluding the extremely maladjusted, there does appear to be a significant relationship between actual job situations, defense mechanisms, and problem resolution. Most distressed workers are not extremely maladjusted but are treated as though they are. Sooner or later, their behavior reflects their colleagues' perceptions of them. Much of the plight of distressed workers stems from the inability of their supervisors and coworkers to understand and accept them. Many non-distressed workers think that their distressed colleagues are alien people having needs unlike "normal" people. A closer analysis of the agency adjustment patterns of distressed workers shows that it is

not their behavior that is abnormal but their opportunities to behave as normal people. Distressed helpers have the following needs:

THE NEED NOT TO BE LOVED TO DEATH. Distressed
workers do not need misplaced kindness; instead, they need empathetic, but fair, guidance. Often, colleagues and supervisors try
to make up for a worker's problems by giving him or her unearned
rewards. No matter how well intended, unearned promotions and
busy work jobs cause additional problems. With so much emphasis
currently being placed on understanding and assisting people in
trouble, it is easy for human service agency personnel to engage in
overcompensatory actions. This may lead to the *distressed worker
syndrome.*

The distressed worker syndrome refers to the process by
which workers use their points of distress (e.g. gender, age or ethnic differences, alcoholism, and mental and terminal illnesses) to
beat the system. "When I want to get out of doing an assignment,"
a female worker confided, "I just tell my male supervisor that I'm
having 'female problems.'" This is beating the system by not doing
the required work. Using their personal distress as a crutch, they
hobble through work, manipulating their perceived oppressors
(other agency personnel). Another worker said, "If I want to leave
early and beat the traffic, I tell my boss that we old folks need to
get on the road before the kids get out there." Few workers in this
category are seeking to optimize their contributions to their agencies. Instead, they only seek to minimize complications during
their employment.

To the worker who knows that he or she is not putting forth
the required effort but is receiving positive sanctions, success
based on merit is a meaningless concept. Yet using the old maxim
that the shortest distance between two points is a straight line,
many workers—well adjusted and maladjusted—are content to
"slide by" with a minimum effort. Making it easy for ethnic minorities, women, older workers, alcoholics, and the other workers
discussed in this book to slide by also makes it easy to deny them
promotions.

THE NEED TO RECEIVE CONSISTENT TREATMENT. Too
often, supervisors and colleagues assume that distressed workers
are also of lower intelligence. Along with this assumption goes the

belief that distressed workers do not know the difference between properly executed and improperly executed assignments. As a result, they frequently are talked to as if they were children. Furthermore, rewards and punishments are capricously given to them. Unlike loving them to death, supervisors and colleagues using this technique are thwarting distressed workers' desire to compete for success. "Why bother," a dejected worker frowned, "when they feel like giving me praise, they will. When they don't, they won't." He was referring to colleagues who praised him for a similar report that he was criticized for this time.

Feeling confused and powerless, many distressed workers give up and sink deeper into the mire of mediocrity; others retire on the job. Good work and bad work become synonymous with wasted work. If enough coworkers and supervisors respond this way, distressed workers do not drop out: they are pushed out!

THE NEED IS TO BE ACCEPTED AS A FELLOW HUMAN BEING. Distressed workers need supervisors and coworkers who can touch, smell, laugh, and cry with them. Coworkers who view them as being highly contagious disease germs consciously or subconsciously seek to avoid contact with them. "These people are as phony as a three-dollar bill," a rejected worker observed. The best way to help a distressed colleague is not by giving an "I understand your problems" lecture and then behaving otherwise. Distressed or not, all workers need colleagues who: (1) will be honest in evaluating their work, (2) will tell them what they are doing wrong and what they need to do to improve, and (3) will assist them in their efforts to improve themselves or their job situation.

Helpers who are defined by their colleagues as being "troublemakers" or "in trouble" have the statistically least probable chance of succeeding to become or remain an integral member of their organizations. Social practitioners often use the difficulty of the situation as an excuse for not getting involved when a fellow helper needs help. Few people doubt the importance of human service personnel, but many doubt their ability or willingness to help ailing or disgruntled colleagues. This, then, has been a plea for helpers to practice within their own ranks what they liberally and successfully do outside it: help each other to realize their optimum potentials.

EXERCISE DRILL

Interventions

1. Paul comes to you for help. He falsely believes that his other coworkers are trying to get him fired. They are, he states, spreading lies about him and his family. Other workers have told him that this is not true. What will you do?

_____

_____

_____

_____

2. Eloise makes you angry when she whines about work conditions that you also agree need changing. She is a very sensitive person who does not accept criticism gracefully. In her usual whining voice she asks you for advice. What will you do?

_____

_____

_____

_____

3. Alvin stops you in the hall and tells you that he has a personal crisis that must be resolved in a couple of days. You are late to a meeting with a client. This is the first time that Alvin has taken you up on your offer to help him anytime he needs you. What will you do?

_____

_____

_____

_____

4. Belinda is having an affair with another woman. She is very much concerned that if her supervisor finds out it will cost her a promotion. You feel very uncomfortable talking about homosexuality but also realize that Belinda needs someone to talk to. She doesn't want you to tell her what to do; she only wants to "get some things off my chest." What will you do?

_____

_____

_____

_____

5. Jason has lost all desire to be an integral part of your agency's informal structure. He comes to work, does what is expected of him, and leaves the other workers alone. He almost never joins in informal small-group talks. Recently, you noticed your own tendency to talk to others about Jason when he is close by. When you apologized to him for your behavior, he said, "That's okay. It doesn't bother me. Besides, I don't have time to waste talking to people about petty things." The next day, Betty approaches you and starts to talk about Jason's refusal to participate in the office party. At that moment, Jason moves to a work station a few feet from where you and Betty are talking. What will you do?

_____

_____

_____

_____

6. Marsha is a new employee who has a history of quitting jobs whenever other workers try to establish close relationships with her. She is a loner. She is assigned to your work unit in which team members must trust each other and establish a close professional relationship if they are to successfully help clients. What will you do?

_____

_____

_____

_____

7. Richard drinks alcoholic beverages on the job and admits to you, his supervisor, that he does it to irritate his coworkers. He is not an alcoholic. Furthermore, he is one of the most productive workers you supervise, but he also is an obnoxious person. What will you do?

_____

_____

_____

_____

8. Marilyn seeks your counsel regarding her behavior, but whenever you try to give her feedback, she changes the subject.
   What will you do?

_____

_____

_____

9. Nathan is ambivalent about his behavior. Some days he wants
   to change it and other days the same behavior is fine. You are
   his friend and he asks your advice. What will you do?

_____

_____

_____

10. Patricia swears that God has told her how to solve the prob-
    lems of the world. As a colleague, she would like for you to
    arrange for her to meet with the governor of your state. What
    will you do?

_____

_____

_____

Possible Helpful Responses

1. Delusions are real to those who have them. Do not argue with
   Paul and do not agree with him, as either action is likely to reinforce his delusion. You can, however, let him know that you
   understand that he believes his colleagues are plotting against
   him, but this does not seem true to you.

2. Helpers do get angry and to pretend that you are not will prevent you from using your anger in a constructive manner. Let

Eloise know that you agree with her appraisal of the situation, but her whining irritates you and perhaps other people too. Then, if she still wants your suggestions, explore with her some viable options that she and/or both of you can take to resolve the work situation. By recognizing your own anger and dealing with it, you can also be more helpful in getting Eloise to deal with her anger.

3. Keep your appointment with the client. Schedule a time that is mutually agreeable for you to talk with Alvin. Your client should not have the appointment cancelled in order for you to talk with Alvin.

4. Do not encourage people to talk about things if you are uncomfortable with their feelings. Furthermore, it would not be helpful to encourage Belinda to express her feeling just for catharsis. Expression of feeling without a consideration of action steps is seldom therapeutic. It may be more helpful for you to refer Belinda to someone who is not uncomfortable talking about homosexuality and can be more active in the problem-solving process.

5. When colleagues withdraw from social interaction, it does not necessarily mean that they do not care about their coworkers. Talking *past* or *about* a person is dehumanizing no matter how "unconcerned" he or she claims to be. If you feel you cannot talk to Jason with Betty, then either don't talk about his refusal to attend the party or move to another place and gossip.

6. Introduce yourself and offer to meet with Marsha to explain team goals and member expectations. Be clear in pointing out to her the necessity for developing a *close, professional* relationship. Answer any questions she has about the team and its members. Encourage team-sharing activities with Marsha, but make it clear to all parties that she will be allowed to blend in at a pace comfortable to her. Tell her what she is doing if you see her rejecting other team members and vice versa.

7. First, let Richard know that drinking on the job will not be tolerated. Second, help him to see that his behavior is both disruptive and dysfunctional. Third, explore with him some other ways of resolving his negative feelings toward his colleagues.

8. Tell Marilyn how her flight-taking affects you. Suggest that she ask for your observations only when she is ready and able to receive them without changing the subject. However, make it clear to her that your friendship is not dependent on discussing her behavior.

9. Tell Nathan what you see him doing, i.e. wavering in regard to the behavior he wants to adopt. Do not confront him with his behavior and suggest or demand an immediate resolution. Rather, let him know that you are aware of his struggle and are willing to assist in any way he may find helpful. Of course, Nathan, not you, must choose and carry out whatever action he deems important.

10. Patricia needs help. Refer her to an appropriate agency or clinician. Tell her supervisor about the conversation.

REFERENCES

1. Jung, C.G.: Civilization in Transition. (Vol. 10 in *Collected Works of Carl Jung.* Edited by G. Adler, et al.) Princeton, NJ: Princeton University Press, 1959–68, pp. 64–65, vol. 10.
2. Jung, C.G.: *The Undiscovered Self.* New York: Mentor, 1957, pp. 16–20.
3. Nicoll, M.: *Psychological Commentaries.* London: Vincent Stuart & John M. Watkins, 1964, pp. 149–50.
4. Rogers, C.R.: *On Becoming a Person.* Boston: Houghton Mifflin, 1961, p. 31.
5. Buber, M.: *The Way of Response.* New York: Schocken Books, 1966, p. 132.
6. Storr, A.: *The Integrity of Personality.* New York: Atheneum, 1961, pp. 41-43.
7. Allport, G.W.: *The Nature of Prejudice.* Garden City, NJ: Doubleday, 1958, p. 346.
8. Gordon, J.E.: *Personality and Behavior.* New York: Macmillan, 1963, p. 497.
9. Menninger, K.: *The Human Mind.* New York: Alfred A. Knopf, 1930, p. 3.
10. Glasser, W.: *Reality Therapy.* New York: Harper & Row, 1965, p. 6.
11. May, R.: *Man's Search for Himself.* New York: W.W. Norton, 1953, pp. 174, 179.

INDEX

181